Advance praise for *The Space Between the Stars*

'A tender, touching and at times bloody funny meditation on life. And death. And how to live. Naidoo explores ways to confront and overcome tragedy by engaging in the simplest, most rewarding things life has to offer. *The Space Between the Stars* is a little treasure. I am richer for having read it.'

DAVID WENHAM

'The world is crying out for more intimate and granular paths through the landscape of grief right now. Thank you, dear Indira, for taking our hand and bravely showing us how being in nature can provide the way.'

SARAH WILSON, AUTHOR OF *THIS ONE WILD AND PRECIOUS LIFE*

'A powerfully moving and insightful journey. Careful attention is a form of love, and Indira Naidoo's vivid writing shows us how such love can lift and expand our minds and spirits, drawing us into the wonders of the universe.'

DAVID GEORGE HASKELL, AUTHOR OF PULITZER FINALIST *THE FOREST UNSEEN*, AND BURROUGHS MEDALLIST *THE SONGS OF TREES*

'This book is life-changing. From deep loss and despair, there is also light. Put your face toward it – it may be the only thing that feels real in this time. Let nature do its job and fix what has been broken in all of us.'

KATE CEBERANO

'Indira Naidoo's writing beats with the strength and power of love and hope, and is a moving meditation on the solace and healing we find in the natural world.'

HOLLY RINGLAND, AUTHOR OF *THE LOST FLOWERS OF ALICE HART*

'Part memoir, part requiem, part journalistic meditation on the natural world ... Naidoo has penned a beautiful reflection on grief, and the unexpected pathway she took to overcome it.'

CHRIS TAYLOR, LOGIE AWARD–WINNING SCRIPTWRITER AND COMEDIAN

The
Space
Between
The
Stars

murdoch books
Sydney | London

The Space Between The Stars

On love, loss and
the magical power
of nature to heal

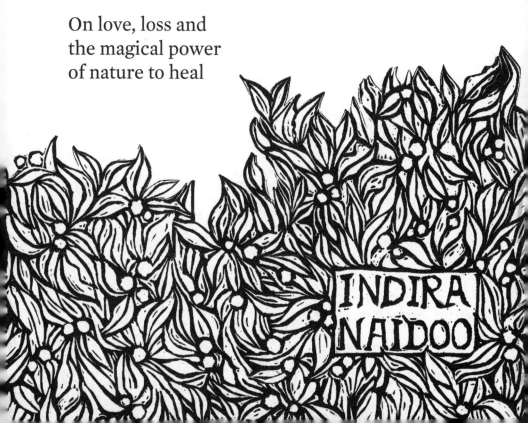

INDIRA NAIDOO

Published in 2022 by Murdoch Books, an imprint of Allen & Unwin

Murdoch Books Australia
83 Alexander Street, Crows Nest NSW 2065
Phone: +61 (0)2 8425 0100
murdochbooks.com.au
info@murdochbooks.com.au

Murdoch Books UK
Ormond House, 26–27 Boswell Street, London WC1N 3JZ
Phone: +44 (0) 20 8785 5995
murdochbooks.co.uk
info@murdochbooks.co.uk

A catalogue record for this book is available from the National Library of Australia

A catalogue record for this book is available from the British Library

ISBN 978 1 92235 161 6

Cover and text design by Trisha Garner
Cover artwork by Clare Walker
Author photo courtesy of Blackfella Films
Typeset by Midland Typesetters, Australia
Printed and bound in Australia by Griffin Press

We acknowledge that we meet and work on the traditional lands of the Cammeraygal people of the Eora Nation and pay our respects to their elders past, present and future.

10 9 8 7 6 5 4 3 2 1

MIX
Paper from responsible sources
FSC® C009448

The paper in this book is FSC® certified. FSC® promotes environmentally responsible, socially beneficial and economically viable management of the world's forests.

For Alia

Author's note

This book touches on grief and suicide, and I invite you to read it with self-care. If any of the stories I share raise issues for you or someone you know, I encourage you to reach out for support.

Indira

Contents

Prologue:	In the beginning	1
Chapter 1:	Stargirl	3
Chapter 2:	Exit wound	7
Chapter 3:	Mooks	17
Chapter 4:	Under the Milky Way	21
Chapter 5:	Aiya's sari and the curtains	31
Chapter 6:	Tree of life	37
Chapter 7:	Cricket	49
Chapter 8:	Birds of a feather	55
Chapter 9:	Highland dancing	67
Chapter 10:	On a wing and a prayer	75
Chapter 11:	Ice cream and apartheid	87

Chapter 12:   Weeds in the cracks   95

Chapter 13:   Peas in a pod   105

Chapter 14:   The shape of things   111

Chapter 15:   Smiley hairclip and birthday party   117

Chapter 16:   Garden in the sky   125

Chapter 17:   Dad's toupee   131

Chapter 18:   The secret life of puddles   137

Chapter 19:   Driving   147

Chapter 20:   High as a kite   155

Chapter 21:   Fortieth and surprise wedding   163

Chapter 22:   Ants in your pants   169

Chapter 23:   Uber goodbye   177

Epilogue: Dust to dust   187

Acknowledgements   191

In the Beginning

This is a story of love and loss – and the joy that can be found just around the corner.

For as long as I can remember there has always been just the three of us – me, Dreamcatcher and Stargirl. Three sisters. Only a year between each. Three peas in a pod. Inseparable. *That's what everybody says.* It's been like this for almost fifty years.

I'm the eldest, the leader of the pack, bossy and extroverted. Dreamcatcher is the middle one, fiercely loyal, the conciliator, kind and gentle. Stargirl is the youngest, the dark outlier, the brilliant non-conformist. We are so tight even our parents can't break our bonds. They hover in the wings, rushing in now and then to rearrange the set or take the play on the road, but for most of the action they sit in the audience.

The regular upheavals in our transglobal childhood knit us even tighter. Another school, another city, another country. It matters not. We are all we need. Until now.

On a chilly autumn's night, Stargirl walked out into her suburban backyard and took her life.

There was no note. No explanation.

How had it come to this?

She was a mother and a wife, a Walkley Award–winning journalist with a Master's degree, a media adviser to state premiers. What had compelled her to end a life I imagine others would *give* their life to live?

For Dreamcatcher and me the stars went dark that night.

Is it possible to ever heal a tear in your universe? Can three now become two?

The pages that follow chart my search to find the light again in the dark places . . .

. . . And how a wise old tree helped me put myself back together.

CHAPTER 1

Stargirl

The memory slices through me like a hot knife.

There's a blanket of cloud across a big grey sky. The air is crackling with an approaching storm. A lawnmower drones in the distance. A bunch of rowdy kids ride past on their dragster bikes. We burst through the back door, pushing against each other excitedly as we race to the pool. Our skin is covered in delicious goosebumps. Me, Dreamcatcher and Stargirl.

We've had to coax Dreamcatcher out of the house. She says it's too cold to swim but we don't care. Stargirl and I scramble up the metal ladder and leap into the icy depths, gasping and squealing as the cold rises through our bodies. Dreamcatcher follows tentatively and tests the sub-zero water with her toe. She releases a melodramatic screech. *You're both maaaaaaaad!* she protests as she scoots back inside, the flyscreen door squeaking on its hinges behind her.

Ha . . . Yes, we are mad.

I squeeze my eyes shut and use my headband as a makeshift blindfold. *I'll be Marco,* I say. *Okay!* she says. *Marco?* I say. *Polo,* she replies. I lunge unsteadily towards the direction of her voice and, like a zombie, grope with my arms extended, but she's already dipped under the surface, barely making a splash. She's always been a fish in water. Fluid, sinuous, streamlined. Even in a small backyard pool she can elude me.

Marco? I say again, straining my ears for any sound that may give away her position. *Polo!* she says just behind me. I swivel around quickly but she's anticipated my pounce and sidesteps me like a nimble boxer in a ring. Damn. *Marco?* I say again, getting annoyed. *Polo!* she shouts back from the other side of the pool, giggling. I lunge again and her smooth, slippery skin slithers past just beyond my fingertips. She picks up the pace. She's darting and swerving like a shimmering King George whiting evading a predator. One moment she's in front of me, the next, suddenly behind. *Polo! Polo! Polo!* she taunts, teasing me in that singsong voice only little sisters deploy.

She seems to surround me from every direction, moving faster and faster. I'm spinning like a crazed dervish. I can feel the ripples of her body in the water. She's cleverly created a whirlpool of choppy waves. I can't keep my balance. I'm feeling dizzy. A foreboding chill descends as the pool closes in. And then the air goes still.

Is her breathing getting heavier? Yes, her movements are getting slower, more laboured.

Marco? I say, sensing my prey is tiring. But there's no response, only the gentle lick and slap of the water against the pool wall. *Marco?* I repeat, concern now rising in my voice. Still nothing. *Where is she?* I hold my breath and strain my ears. But all I can hear is my pounding heartbeat. I rip off my blindfold in a panic, scan the pool and then dive down, searching for her. Shards of grey light pierce the rocking water. The chlorine stings my eyes but I force them to open wider as I peer through the murky haze. I see her yellow hairclip glinting on the pool floor but there's no sign of her. Anywhere.

I gasp and swallow a mouthful of water and come back up to the surface coughing and spluttering. I stand, head just above the surface, and throw my arms over the side of the pool, heaving with exhaustion and confusion.

And then I see her. Leaning against the wall near the back door, bent over with laughter. I've put on a great show for her – groping stupidly in a blindfold for someone who isn't there. She doesn't care that I think she may have drowned. Of course she doesn't.

I'm going to get you, I say, dripping down the pool ladder with as much menace as a ten-year-old can muster. She runs into the kitchen feigning terror. *Mum! Indira said she's going to get me. MUUUHmm . . .!*

That's Stargirl. Rarely playing by the rules. Enigmatic. Ethereal. Constructing her own cosmos. A Houdini you can never pin down. Everywhere and nowhere. Closer than your shadow, as remote and unreachable as a distant sun.

But one day she *will* be gone, sooner than her time, exploding in a blinding supernova that will shatter our universe.

You see, stars never go quietly. They suck you into their black hole.

CHAPTER 2

Exit Wound

With just one phone call my world has gone dark.

It's like being blasted by an atomic wave – the impact hurtling me out of myself in violent slow motion. I've been flung through the air like a floundering crash-test dummy with no airbag to save me.

I've landed with a thud, buried alive in a bleak nuclear winter, the radioactive fallout settling around me like deadly fluttering snowflakes. The calcium is leaching from my bones. There's a black chasm where my rib cage used to be. I can put my hand right through myself.

A suffocating silence would have been tolerable but not this. There's a guttural howling in my head. Tortured cries. Anguished wails. Smothered whimpers. I don't recognise the voice but I know it belongs to me. I didn't know loss could trigger a sonic assault like this, from within. An incessant, moaning, discordant sonata only I can hear.

The next morning, I pull open the curtains to face the first day without her.

I'm blinded by dazzling sunshine. It's incandescent. Almost indecent. This is the cruel trick grief plays on you. For the rest of the world the day is humming with happiness. The Sydney breeze is carrying the excited strains of schoolgirl chatter; a squark of cockatoos conspires on a nearby rooftop. In the distance the Rose Bay ferry chugs around Garden Island churning up a foaming white trail. And on our balcony my husband Mark is watering the calendulas. They're bobbing and bowing, offering their bright-yellow faces for a sunny autumn's kiss.

But there's a thick smear of Vaseline over my lens. And not in a good Doris Day–matinee kind of way. The world is blurry and fogged over, and no adjusting the dials can bring it back into focus. It's like the morning after a boozy jaunt in the old Kings Cross. Remember those? Where you'd give yourself to the night, staggering in ridiculous heels from The Albury to Barons, sharing bar stools with bouncers and hookers, crooks and footballers. Later, there would be memory fragments of a taxi ride home, sucking in cool air through the open window to keep the head-spins at bay, a fumble with house keys, passing out on the couch to the late-night music of *Rage*, only to wake with a cotton-wool head, in a drooly daze, to fuzzy white noise on the telly. *We'll return you to normal programming soon.*

Now the word *normal* feels so inadequate and pathetic. I don't want normal. I want a supernatural force to bring her back from the dead.

I'm overwhelmed by the urge to flee – to throw open my apartment door and just run and run, not to anywhere in particular, just away from myself. To feel the breeze stinging my eyes with hot tears and filling my lungs with life again. If only the inertia weren't so crippling. My legs won't move. *Just put one foot in front of the other. You've done it a million times.* But it's hopeless. I'm a crumpled marionette waiting for a puppeteer to reanimate me. Alone in the universe.

For the briefest of seconds, a fug of confusion plays tricks on me and I forget last night's phone call ever happened. My mind merrily begins checklisting the day I was planning to have ... *Scan my emails, put on the kettle, slice some fruit for breakfast, pay the gas bill, drop off the dry-cleaning, pick up some lamb for dinner* ...

... and then the unbearable darkness of being rushes back, punching me in the gut.

Doubled over, I limp to the bathroom and splash my face with water, careful not to look in the mirror. I'm not ready to see myself yet.

I buckle on my urban armour – leggings, T-shirt, puffer jacket, runners, cap and sunnies – hoping, as I slip out onto the street, that I won't see anyone who knew me yesterday. That was the old me. From today there will always be *that me* and *this me*.

As I stagger unsteadily along Macleay Street a fierce wind is blowing up from the harbour, sending a shiver through the plane trees. I zip up my jacket and plunge my hands deeper into my pockets. On days like these you can see why the early colony harnessed the wind along this ridge to drive its flour mills. Now, helped along by the phalanx of apartment buildings, even on a calm day the Potts Point wind tunnel can drone and rumble like a squadron of B-52s.

I turn the corner into the café strip along Challis Avenue. An agitated queue of socially distanced locals is snaking across the footpath. Their morning-coffee defibrillation can't come fast enough. I spy some neighbours in the line but thankfully they're too preoccupied with their phones to notice the haunted figure scurrying past them. *I will break if anyone asks me how I am.*

I head to the McElhone Stairs, which cut through the ridge down to Woolloomooloo Bay. Locals call these the 'Stairs of Doom', and with good reason. The three flights of 113 steps will reduce all but the fittest to a vacuum bag of gasping. It should get a Heart Foundation tick of approval. Over the centuries, parched sailors and the Bay's working class have made their way up these stairs, enticed by the siren call of the Cross.

As I stumble down, steadying myself on the metal rail, I pass the stair runners doing their chastened morning sprints. I wonder if they know of the lustful footsteps they follow. Or maybe that's the demon they're trying to purge. Perhaps the 'Stairway to Sin' would be more apt.

I cross Cowpers Wharf Road to the fence line of the Garden Island naval base, where a fleet of gunmetal-grey battleships is moored near the Harry's Café de Wheels pie cart. Pieces of stale bread roll have been scattered along the footpath, and a greedy cackle of cockatoos and deferential pigeons is pecking at the unexpected smorgasbord.

In the marina, polished cruisers strain against their moorings, cheek by jowl, glistening like undulating keys on a piano. Behind them, the city's towering skyscape shimmers above the dense tree line of the Royal Botanic Garden. How have I never noticed the prison-guard menace those skyscrapers cast over the city? I can hear the thwack of their batons against the calloused skin of their palms.

I jog up the stairs to Mrs Macquaries Road, through a grove of golden wattle, and follow the dirt track up the slope. The sounds of the city begin to muffle as the trees huddle in closer. Two figbirds are cooing just overhead. Rolling ripples from a boat's backwash lick against the bush rock. And there's another sound . . . I still myself to heighten my senses. Yes . . . I can hear it now . . . just above the sound of my own heartbeat . . . an almost imperceptible whisper in the rustling leaves, willing me to come in deeper. I've heard these murmurings before on my many walks through the Gardens, but this is the first time I am listening, deeply, letting the vibrations travel through me and merge with my insides. I close my eyes as the hum builds into gentle rhythms as old as the earth. I know this area is sacred. Maybe these are the songlines of the Gadigal people. Close to where I'm standing, clans from across the Sydney Basin would gather for male initiation ceremonies. To prove they were ready to become men, boys would endure all manner of arduous trials, including the removal of their upper right incisor.

A place of suffering and a place of regeneration. Is that how I have found myself here?

The she-oaks and the eucalypts lean in closer still. My skin tingles from an unseen embrace. With no words passing between us, these trees seem to intuitively know what I need: openness and enclosure. There's a clearing just ahead, above the Andrew (Boy) Charlton swimming baths, where I sit down on the grass, the smell of damp earth rising through the roots. The numbness in my body begins to melt away like a slow-moving glacier travelling through a rocky fjord. In this stillness there's space to hear my turbulent thoughts. My head is all at sea, shipwrecked on a wild, nightmarish coastline, listing dangerously, inches above the waterline.

As I surrender to the quiet, the torrents of emotion coalesce into the unformed words that have been haunting me: *You were her older sister. It was your job to keep her safe. How could you have failed her so utterly?* The accusation hangs dark and heavy in the morning air as a jogger pounds past on the lower path. I follow the sound of his footfall as he disappears behind a scrubby clump of honey reed.

Something on the ground catches my eye. A spider's web, intricately woven between two blades of grass, quivers in the sunlight. A tiny chandelier of dewdrops hangs from its silken threads. Any other time I would have carelessly trampled over this labour of love. Thankfully, today my fractured heart can sit with its fragile beauty.

A wash of warm light breaks through the leaves. I look up and notice that all the branches above me belong to a solitary tree – a towering Moreton Bay fig encircled by a wooden walkway. Its umbrellaed canopy must spread for more than 20 metres. A dozen muscular limbs radiate from its solid trunk, stretching out along the eastern slope of Mrs Macquaries Road, arching across the hill and over the lower footpath. Its branches are covered with hundreds of waxy, dark-green leaves with brown furry undersides. Light-green fruits hang in clusters. Its surface roots flow in thick ribbons along the ground towards the harbour. The roots are scaly and reptilian, like the claws of a giant slumbering dinosaur. This fig tree is magnificent! It even has a door-shaped hollow in its trunk, completing its fairytale appearance.

I wander over and gently stroke its bark, marvelling at the gnarly texture of the deep ridges and grooves, and how grounded and permanent it feels in contrast to my ghostly presence. I imagine crawling into the hollow and disappearing into a faraway land.

And then, instantly, I see the significance of this startling encounter. It's no accident I have found myself here. I am standing in the protective shade of my ancestral home. Trees were our first refuge from danger. They were where we sought safety from predators and the elements. As children we climbed high into their branches to hide and observe and feel like rulers over our domain.

We are earthly cousins, this tree and I. We may be arranged a little differently, but we are composed of the same molecular elements: carbon, hydrogen and oxygen, metals and minerals. Its branches are my limbs, its bark my skin, its sap my blood. We resuscitate each other with the gift of our breath. I supply its carbon dioxide; it gives me my oxygen. Can two beings be in deeper symbiosis?

Given its size, this silent sentinel has been here quietly supporting my life long before I even knew it existed. Is it now offering itself up as my spirit guide? Sharing its strength and wisdom as I battle my demons and try to glue myself back together?

Here with this tree, secluded in this wedge of nature, I sense I can sit alone yet not feel isolated. I can draw on this tree for a unique form of solace. It will be here but ask nothing of me. I can come to rest and recover without needing to give anything in return. Instead of doing, I can just be. With state and national borders shut for now by Covid-19, marooned from my friends, family and

Exit Wound

grandchildren Jack and Abbie, iso-walks my only form of escape, can this tree and the fragments of urban nature around me lead me out of my grief? *Could nature be my saviour?*

CHAPTER 3

Mooks

It's school holidays. That magical parent-free time when the three sisters can roam untethered – dream, play, lose ourselves in our imaginations. Perhaps we'll ride our dragster bikes down to the local creek, where a posse of neighbourhood kids is already gathering. We'll take turns leaping into the murky currents from a tyre-swing precariously slung over a weeping willow. It gives us rope burns that we parade around like badges of honour. They're added to the other war wounds – the splinters, gashes and grazes – courtesy of the gnarly underwater tree roots and jagged river rocks. Oh, the unadulterated joy of it all! Afterwards – skin tingling from the leached tea-tree oil in the creek water soothing our abrasions – it's back on the bikes, Dreamcatcher and me racing Stargirl home, standing on the pedals for extra speed, the cereal-box rainbow reflectors on the wheel spokes scattering the sunlight in a kaleidoscope of colour.

We skid back into the driveway; bikes are strewn, wheels still spinning as we dash up the back stairs into the kitchen. We raid the fridge, gulp down tall glasses of Tang and fry up some crunchy cheese sandwiches slathered in Worcestershire sauce. The Sony Trinitron kicks into action and we grab a vinyl beanbag each to watch the movie matinee. It's Elvis in *G.I. Blues*, gyrating on an airstrip. Stargirl gives a whoop of delight.

This particular summer, though, our Famous Five adventures have been scuttled. The household is in a state of frenzy. The fridge and freezer are being stocked with strange, exotic animal parts: pig trotters, lamb brains, chicken livers and fish roe. The brassware – including the prayer lamp – is getting a polish on the newspaper-lined dining-room table, bedsheets are being laundered, blankets are airing, the linen cupboard is stacked with new satin-edged embroidered towels.

I'm being turfed out of my room, which doubles as the guest room, to make way for an honoured visitor: Aiya is coming from South Africa.

We've talked to Aiya on the phone long distance several times, but the last time we actually *met* our grandmother, we were just toddlers. Even the grainy Kodak photo of her we've been shown doesn't jog our memories. She doesn't look like any grandmother we've seen before. No grey curls or cuddly demeanour. In the photo, Aiya is posing with our grandfather and some of their nine children. Our mother is one of the little ones in the front row with ringlets. Aiya is only in her late thirties in this photo, but not surprisingly she looks exhausted by her brood. She's wearing a cream sari with a floral maroon border. Her jet-black hair is pulled back tightly in a bun. Severe gold-rimmed glasses pinch the bridge of her nose. Her eyes are saying *Posing for this photo is a waste of my valuable time.*

It's well after midnight when Aiya finally arrives from the airport, her chiffon sari scented with masala. *Ayore!* she exclaims in Tamil as she greets each of us with a rib-crushing hug. Stargirl's chipmunk cheeks get an extra squeeze.

Tea is quickly prepared as Aiya's brown leather suit-cases are unzipped with great reverence in the middle of the living-room floor to reveal her exotic contraband. Carefully wrapped in layers of sari fabric are bags of South African spices . . . there's golden turmeric, earthy cumin, fennel, coriander, garam masala, dried chillies, cinnamon sticks, cardamon pods and cloves. Aiya's a walking spice bazaar.

She has dozens of pretty coloured bangles for us, but it's the bag of murukku that our eyes dart to. These Indian snacks appear only on special occasions. Crunchy, unyielding, deep-fried, ribbony swirls of savoury biscuit deliciousness, flavoured with chilli and caraway seeds. *Don't even attempt them with dentures.*

We are rationed to just one each so the precious murukku can last longer. Dreamcatcher and I adhere to the restrictions, but by the end of the weekend all the murukku have mysteriously vanished. The thief hasn't even tried to cover their tracks. The murukku packet sits empty on the pantry shelf surrounded by a few remnant crumbs and oily fingerprints.

Even before the disciplinary wooden spoon is reached for, Stargirl confesses.

To our indignation no punishment is meted out for this crime against humanity. *She's the baby,* our parents try to justify. Although there's just one year's difference between each of us, Stargirl will continue to be the beneficiary – and the casualty – of being *the baby.*

The legacy of her audacious pantry raids? From that weekend on, Stargirl will be teased mercilessly by the family as *Murukku Girl,* the taunt shortened along the way to just *Mooks.*

At Stargirl's funeral, forty years later, as I stand beside her coffin, the pandemic restricting mourners in the chapel to just twenty wretched souls, I have a flashback to that weekend long ago. *Mooks, I would give you all the murukku in the world just to hear you laugh again.*

CHAPTER 4

Under the Milky Way

I'm wary of sharing this secret with others – fearful of eliciting prickles of envy. So I'll just come out and say it – I've always slept like a baby. Asleep as soon as my head hits the pillow, mostly sleeping right through the night, oblivious to the unsettling street noises around me. Waking the next morning feeling rested and re-energised.

Now, after taking more than half a century of peaceful slumber for granted, it's payback time. Mr Sandman has well and truly deserted me.

Going to bed is like lying down in the dark with an open chest wound. I'm on an operating table. The scene is chaotic. A blinding overhead lamp has been directed at my heart. A frenetic, masked surgical team with panic in their eyes works feverishly around me. They haven't been able to stem the bleeding. The anaesthetic isn't working. I can feel every slice of the scalpel but no one can hear my screams.

This is why my bed has become a dangerous place.

I check the time – 2 am. Moonlight is streaming in through the break in the curtains. Mark is sound asleep beside me. I slip out of bed and walk out onto the balcony, grateful for the cool harbour breeze on my damp skin.

Like most of the world, Potts Point is unnervingly quiet since the pandemic. No hoons revving up their car engines. No late-night revellers spilling out of tiny bars. No rough sleepers having a barney. No cops. No sirens. Not even a yelping dog. It seems everyone is sleeping but me.

Tonight, all I have for company is the cosmos.

The northern sky is inky black, faintly lit by a sliver of moon and a scattering of stars. I imagine Stargirl up there, among them, twinkling in one of those far-flung uncharted galaxies. What does this tiny blue marble look like to her now? Can she even recognise this speck of dust from her new resting place in the Milky Way? Or maybe she has travelled beyond the outer reaches of our known universe, hurtling in a slipstream past countless stars and planets, nebulae and black holes, quarks and quasars, to the final destination of all shooting stars – the Heaven Constellation.

I smile. In moments like these in the past, when I was with Stargirl, both of us in deep contemplation, enjoying the stillness, she would always break the spell by lighting up one of her blasted cigarettes. *Well, wherever she is, I hope they have a smokers' corner.*

Under the Milky Way

As my eyes adjust to the dark expanse, more stars become visible. They're mere pinpricks of light, soft and shimmery. I try to imagine the intensity of those burning suns on the edge of known matter, infernos of such ferocity that I can still see the glow emitted by their balls of fire all these millions of years later. Many would have ceased to exist long before their light even reached me. Their destruction would have been catastrophic for all life in their individual solar systems, just as we would evaporate the second our own sun imploded. Obliteration. Annihilation. Oblivion.

Then again, peering up at these sparkling wonders I can also see the good that can come from endings. Just like Stargirl, their radiance can burn brightly long after they are gone. The glow from their embers can light the way for others and guide travellers on their treacherous crossings.

As long as you can see the stars, you can never truly be lost.

The upside of not being able to sleep much is that my childhood fascination with the night sky has been reignited. I now look forward to my nocturnal stirrings and the new discoveries I am making. Living right up against the Sydney CBD I had always assumed the light pollution from the neon signs would destroy any chance of meaningful stargazing. But even in my topsy-turvy city life where night has become day, the stars never went away.

The Space Between the Stars

I've been scanning the amateur astronomy websites searching for the best place and time to watch the night sky. I'm thrilled to discover I don't even have to leave home! An email from the Northern Suburbs Astronomy Society assures me that from my Potts Point balcony, on a clear night with a good telescope, I should be able to see at least twelve stars, several planets, nebulae and an assortment of satellites and space junk. *A veritable traffic jam up there.*

As Sydney's latest coronavirus stay-at-home lockdown has been briefly suspended, the astronomy society's observing officer, Phil Angilley, has offered to assist me with my first Close Encounter. Phil arrives one evening as a bright, yellow moon hangs in the eastern sky. Mark is working late at the ABC TV studios, so it's just me, Phil and the stars. The conditions are perfect for stargazing. He's armed with all sorts of gadgets. As well as his impressive-looking Meade LX200 telescope, he has a tripod, two steel cases, a GPS unit, and a crate of batteries and cables. I can see he takes this star caper rather seriously.

Phil is in his early sixties. By day he's an unassuming electronics specialist, but at night there's nothing he enjoys more than a tango with his telescope. He fell in love with the stars as a young boy scout, and that wide-eyed, childlike fascination has clearly not left him.

He asks me what's behind *my* interest in the stars.

I hesitate.

What I *really* want to tell him is that it's because there's someone up there I want to find. I want to tell him I'm searching for my youngest sister who took her life on a cold starless night during Melbourne's first long lockdown. I want to tell him that I need to make sure she's safe and warm and has something to eat. I want to tell him I need to find her so I can tell her not to be afraid and that everything is going to be all right. But what I tell him is that I am writing a book about the healing power of nature. This is as much of the truth as I can manage.

We start setting up the equipment on the balcony. Phil attaches the battery to the telescope. The Meade suddenly jumps into action, setting about finding magnetic north – the first plot-point it will need to make its calculations. Phil then punches in GPS data so the telescope can locate the specific night-sky objects we hope to see.

The telescope is like a mad lab scientist, mumbling to itself, buzzing and whirring, gyrating up and down and then swivelling back and forth, seemingly of its own accord. It's like a mini R2-D2. Suddenly it tilts up and stops with a satisfied purr. The Meade has found our first target.

Alpha Centauri is the closest star system to the earth. To the naked eye it appears as just two stars, but with binoculars or a good telescope you can see it actually consists of three stars: Centauri A, Centauri B and Centauri C. *Three stars for three sisters.*

Because it can only be found in the southern sky, it doesn't feature in Greek or Roman mythology, but to the Boorong people of north-western Victoria, Alpha Centauri has a powerful Dreamtime story. They call it Bermbermgl and believe the cluster depicts two courageous brothers who killed an emu in battle. I try to picture this heroic hunt as I squint through the lens and see two brightly glowing orbs and a smaller, dimmer one. It's humbling to think that although these are the stars closest to us, they're still 4.37 light years away.

Crossing this distance is hard to fathom, but I read on astronomy fan pages that with new experimental forms of travel currently being developed, such as 'nuclear pulse propulsion' and 'laser light sail' technology, the time it takes could be reduced to mere decades. The Trekkie in me wants to believe – and here, right now, under this ethereal dome, the magic casts its spell.

There's a buzz and a whirr. R2-D2 has found something else for us. The Beehive Cluster. I peer into the lens and see a swarm of tiny sparkles. The Beehive sits within the Cancer constellation and comprises as many as 1000 stars. In 1769, Charles Messier, an influential French astronomer, added the cluster to his famous guidebook of nebulous objects. Phil talks about Messier's guide in reverential tones. *The original Hitchhiker's Guide to the Galaxy.*

Peering at the cluster through a telescope is like watching a fireworks explosion on New Year's Eve.

Under the Milky Way

The colours and the pulses are like an intergalactic celebration. *If only I had known there was another 'nightlife' I could have escaped to after two alcohol-related fatalities all but shut down Sydney's inner-city nightlife on the ground.*

The next stargazing spectacle R2 has found for us is the Orion Nebula, familiar to almost everyone. Even if you don't know it by name, you would no doubt have seen images of this famous celestial body. I remember as a teenager blu-tacking a glossy poster of it up on my bedroom wall. There was also a worn print in our school science lab. The Orion Nebula is part of the 'sword of Orion' in the Orion constellation. Orion is known as the Saucepan in Australia, and the sword is referred to as its handle. The sword shimmers around its middle star. I can see this formation on most clear nights, but through a telescope I can almost touch it. It's pulsating with energy and vibrancy, its mottled surface interspersed with dancing tendrils.

The Orion Nebula is the rock star of all nebulae due to its closeness to earth and its haunting greenish hue. It's as if someone has splashed a shot glass of absinthe against a bar wall, leaving a psychedelic glow in the sky. And its size leaves the mind boggling as well: 24 light years in diameter. *Now that's some trip.*

Phil tells me that nebulae are found in the huge expanse of dust and gas near stars. They are bubbling cauldrons of unimaginable force and pressure where stars are synthesised – *a nursery of sorts, if you like.*

I'm learning that stargazing is as much a religious experience as a scientific one. So it's not surprising that many priests are credited alongside astronomers with star discoveries. *Surely only an omnipotent force could have been responsible for this level of design perfection.*

I ask Phil about the gaps between the celestial bodies – the 'space between the stars'. *Will we be looking at these?* Phil seems genuinely surprised. *They're the boring bits,* he says. *Why would you want to know about those? It's just dust and helium and hydrogen – and more hydrogen. Don't you want to focus on the stars and planets where the main action is?* Phil has a point. I'm not sure why I'm drawn to these overshadowed places. Maybe it's because they form the backdrop that allows everything else to shine. *All stars need a support act, right?*

The space between the stars is technically known as the interstellar medium. It's the primordial pond where everything gets created. Stars – and the nebulae that form them – have their beginnings here. The interstellar medium is really a supercharged space hurricane, swirling with ions, atoms, molecules, dust grains, electromagnetic radiation, cosmic rays and magnetic fields, held in perfect suspension. Like a ballet dancer gracefully balancing on the tip of her toe – too much propulsion and she will topple, not enough lift and the illusion cannot be sustained.

Under the Milky Way

As my own inner world swirls off kilter, I realise I am peering at a universe that's explosive, yes, but with the delicately calibrated tension of a harp string. Proof that equilibrium and turbulence can coexist in harmony.

Buzz . . . whirr . . . swivel . . . a little to the right . . . tilt up . . . and presto! The last star the Meade telescope finds for us is Betelgeuse. This red supergiant is in the Orion constellation – and it's a beauty! As my eye finds focus, I spot a blazing sphere with a fiery orange-red corona, 1000 times the size of our sun. Even though it burns with such potency, Betelgeuse, Phil tells me, is dying. It's nearing the end of its life, and the science fraternity is excitedly preparing for what that explosion might look like.

When a massive star like this runs out of nuclear material in its core, it collapses under its own gravity and turns into a supernova. *Supernova.* It sounds grandly poetic, but is it just another way of describing how a star ends its own life? *Is a supernova a suicide on a colossal scale?*

Researchers have estimated that Betelgeuse will run out of puff within the next 100,000 years – far into the future when measured in human years, but to a star just the blink of an eye. The explosion will be so immense it will briefly outshine an entire galaxy.

Is that what happened in my own small universe when Stargirl collapsed under the weight of her own gravity? Maybe my world hasn't gone dark at all. Perhaps the reverse has happened. Could I have been irradiated with so much pure light that I've been temporarily blinded by its intensity and truthfulness?

My evening of stargazing with Phil has shown me the infinite wonders of the night sky. All I need to do is look up occasionally. I am not the first collection of molecules to occupy this space-time continuum – and I certainly won't be the last. My life doesn't represent even a nano-second of existence, but rather than this leaving me feeling small and insignificant, tonight I feel gladiatorial, heroic, undefeated.

I realise I could endlessly scour this infinite expanse, looking into dark places that even light struggles to illuminate, searching for the reason why Stargirl is gone. Even the gods can't be expected to decipher the unfathomable. I am trying to solve a murder mystery no detective could ever crack. And that's because it's not a whodunnit but a *why*dunnit. The victim was the assailant.

Just above me, in the right-hand pocket of the sky, near North Head, a satellite zips over Watsons Bay and disappears behind the horizon. The headlands are backlit with a deep magenta glow. Sunrise is approaching.

What will the new day hold? What will the new day heal?

Perhaps Stargirl's supernova should be seen as a form of divine chaos. A reminder that like the stars, we are all made up of energy in constant flux, changing shape and structure, moving from the dark into the light, creating and destroying. Not forever. Just for eternity.

CHAPTER 5

Aiya's Sari and the Curtains

We're fascinated by Aiya. She rarely speaks to us, and when she does it is usually to scold or discipline. Are we really this naughty?

After her morning shower each day, Aiya goes through an elaborate dressing ritual. She lets us sit on the bed and watch.

We're surprised by how long her hair is when she releases her French roll. Cascading, dyed-black, wavy tendrils drop all the way to her waist. She gives her hair long, firm strokes with her brush and rubs some coconut oil through the ends. She then expertly wraps her locks back into a firm bun at the nape of her neck and secures it in place with several long, black hairpins. We've never seen an old person with such long hair. We ask her how old she is. *Fifty-six*, she says. *That's ancient*, Stargirl says.

Dreamcatcher shoots her an admonishing look, but Aiya laughs for the first time since she arrived. *None of us know then that fifty-six is an age Stargirl will never reach.*

Next Aiya picks up a small, dark-blue glass bottle and pours some moisturiser into her hand. The lotion is runny and pink (the colour of musk stick candy). It makes her ebony skin glisten. *Oil of Olay*, she explains. *It keeps my skin soft.* Her eyes suddenly darken and her voice drops to a whisper. *Put cream on your body every day, girls*, she says as though sharing a secret people take to their grave. Based on their youthful looks, it's a beauty ritual most of her children and grandchildren have embraced wholeheartedly. (Years later, I discover that Oil of Olay was developed in Durban, South Africa, near Pieter-maritzburg where Aiya lived and where we were born. In fact, Oil of Olay became such a local success story, thanks to devotees such as Aiya, that Olay went on to become a global beauty brand.)

Now Aiya slips on a long cream cotton petticoat and ties it firmly on her hip, which pushes her belly out over the top in a gentle roll. She puts on a tight cropped navy cotton blouse and secures the hooks along the bodice.

Then she selects a sari to wear for the day. We want her to put on the blue one with a wide gold embroidered border but she says that's only for special occasions. Today is a busy day of chores: there's the laundry to do and home-made lime pickles to bottle, so a practical sari is selected. It's a plain cream one with a maroon border, which falls in soft gossamer folds.

The sari is a long rectangular piece of fabric that seems to go on for eternity. This is the magic part. Aiya tucks one end into her petticoat and attaches it in place with a large safety pin. She then grabs a metre of fabric and expertly gathers it into pleats, which she secures with another pin. Then she begins wrapping the fabric around her hip, pulling it firmly as she twists around. Round and round she goes until there are just a few metres left, which she folds over her shoulder and secures to her top with yet another pin.

She looks like a princess!

Never one to dawdle, Aiya sashays out of the room looking immaculate, and heads to the kitchen – the room in every house she spends most of her time in.

After our showers, Dreamcatcher has gone to a neighbour's house, so Stargirl and I decide to sneak back into Aiya's room. We put on some of her Oil of Olay and play with her soft hairbrush, lifting our hair up in tiny French rolls.

We model in front of the mirror, imagining ourselves in a glamorous sari. Why *imagine* when we're standing next to almost the real thing? Thick sapphire-blue brocade curtains hang on the windows of the guest room. They match the bedspread on the double bed. Mum has had them specially made, with strict instructions they are not to be touched by little children.

Stargirl and I grab a side of curtain each and begin twisting ourselves inside the fabric. It feels soft and silky against our skin. We tuck some of the folds into the waist of our jeans and arrange some of the fabric over our shoulders as we pretend to be Aiya. Stargirl mimics Aiya kneeling and praying with her eyes closed in front of a Hindu sami lamp. I pretend to put on some lipstick and a red dot on my forehead. *Ayore! Ayore!* we say, giving our head a little bobble-head shake as Aiya does.

We are having so much fun pretending to be Aiya that we tug and pull at the curtain harder to release more fabric so we can create more pleats. We begin twirling and dancing, losing ourselves in giddy laughter. We imagine that we're dressed in our sari curtains ready to attend a glamorous dinner where everyone will be wearing mink coats and diamonds. We'll be driven there in long stretch limousines by chauffeurs in tuxedos and top hats.

As we shimmy up the stairs to the ballroom everyone will marvel at our stunning saris, not realising they are curtains. Photographers will take our photos. We'll be in all the social pages. *The Naidoo girls in their striking saris.* Boys will line up to dance with us but we'll only dance with each other. Boys are smelly and are hopeless at playing elastics.

Arms clasped around each other's waist, Stargirl and I will twirl and spin across the ballroom floor lifted by the music, twisting faster and faster as the orchestra's violinists rise to their feet. The light from the golden chandeliers will bounce off our saris, turning them into lagoons of liquid turquoise.

Ah, the joy and the freedom! Stargirl breaks away leaping into the air, arms extended like butterfly wings. The crowd roars and gasps as she spins on her toes like an ice skater, the sari curtain clinging tightly to her like a second skin.

And then there's an almighty crash.

We've pulled the wooden curtain rail off its brackets and it has collapsed on us mid dance routine. We've fallen like flattened ballerinas in a mangled curtsy. The downed curtain rail has made a godawful noise, which of course brings the adults running from the four quarters of the house. They burst into the room to find Stargirl and me entangled in curtains, splintered wooden railings and pieces of broken ceiling plaster.

Our backs and shoulders have been bruised in the impact, but there is no sympathy for our wounds once it is established we have no head injuries. We are subjected to a yelling we are sure children can hear all the way to Kathmandu, and instructed to tidy the mess and help put up a bedsheet across the window until the curtains can be repaired.

We are then made to apologise to Aiya, for being in her room without her permission and for touching her things. We are also reminded how important it is to respect our elders and that one day, when we are both Aiyas, we'll understand how naughty our behaviour has been today.

The Space Between the Stars

Of course, it should be the natural course of things that one day we will both be Aiyas, sharing stories and playing with our grandchildren.

For Stargirl, though, that was not to be written in the stars.

CHAPTER 6

Tree of Life

Grief is such a solitary affliction. No two people feel it the same way. Even when it involves the same event or the same person, you're trapped in a torment tailor-made for you.

It's like witnessing an armed hold-up in a 7-Eleven. All the customers have been terrorised by the same gunman, with the same gun, but depending on your proximity, the aisle you happen to be in, even how long you've been in the store, your version of events will vary – frustrating the attending police officers no end.

So the gunman was wearing a balaclava?

Who said that? No . . . no . . . he had a black baseball cap on.

And the scar . . . right cheek or left cheek?

Scar? No . . . he didn't have a scar. He had a tattoo on his neck.

And he was brandishing a sawn-off shotgun, right?

No, it was a knife. It was definitely a knife.

Okay . . . and this man . . . he was about 5 foot 5, correct?

Yeah . . . quite small which is why – on second thoughts – it may have been a woman . . .

Take it from me. Those gripped by grief make unreliable witnesses. The only thing everyone seems to agree on is that something happened. What that *something* is, gets further distorted by the trickery of time. Yesterday, today and tomorrow all merge into the same monster holding you captive, chained, in a suffocating cave, deep within the bowels of the earth. Even when you attempt an escape and start crawling towards the light, the chain around your ankle gets yanked tight, sucking you into the past. The pain cannot end because it is yet to begin.

The unrelenting rain of the last week, fed by the heated oceans, hasn't helped my spirits. Climate crisis, apocalyptic predictions, nature venting its fury. The turmoil outside has mirrored my insides. Wild winds and downpours of biblical proportions have lashed the east coast. *Never seen anything like it,* they've been saying. *Once in a century.* The TV news stories replay in my head in a disturbing loop. When you're nursing a splintered heart, you're more vulnerable to the pain of others. The distressing images trigger my trauma. An entire weatherboard house sucked up in the rising floodwaters, wrenched from its foundations, bobbing in the torrents like a toy in a bathtub. Marooned farm animals, coats muddy and matted, shivering in stranded paddocks. An exhausted grazier, whose eyes had seen everything until now, breaking down in front of the cameras, his weathered face in his rugged hands. He knows he's not coming back from this.

Relief finally comes a week later. There's a break in the weather. The clouds are no longer angry. The sky smiles big and blue. And the sun does its best to tempt me outside again. I inspect the damage to my little balcony garden. A couple of upturned pots, some wind-burnt leaves and a few damaged tomatoes. Luckily it has escaped serious injury.

What has not fared so well is the blue, jewelled expanse I gaze out onto every day. Sydney Harbour is the colour of mud. It looks exhausted and swollen from the tears of a nation in climate denial. *I feel its heartbreak.*

Other parts of my urban backyard seem to have relished the rain. Beyond the naval fleet, across Woolloomooloo Bay – Sydney's Royal Botanic Garden is bursting with vigour. The grassy slopes are a vibrant green and the trees seem to have expanded from the deluge.

Why does seeing that wedge of green wildness make my battered heart soar so? Many others are fascinated by this question. One of the books keeping me company on my morning walks has been *Healing Spaces: The Science of Place and Well-being* by American neuro-immunologist Dr Esther Sternberg. She believes the restorative impact

of nature has much to do with the colour *green* itself.
Our yellow-green vision was the first to evolve. Green
sits roughly in the middle of the light spectrum, not at
the edges, making it more relaxing for our brain to
process the visual information. The more greenery
around us, the calmer we feel. Green also signifies abundance and fertility . . . think oases, lagoons, fern-fringed
waterholes. It was where we knew we would find food
and water. A sanctuary where we could be safe. *Green is
hardwired into our DNA.*

My eyes continue along the tree line, admiring the
seductive, bushy curves of Mrs Macquaries Point. There
are no straight lines in nature, unlike our linear, machine-
built structures. Nature is all about contours and arcs,
twists and waves, flows and meanders. It allows the eye
to duck and weave, catch a glimpse, make a discovery,
something revealed, something hidden. A temptress with
a beguiling promise.

I pause on a slab of ochre-streaked sandstone,
admiring how it hangs in weathered folds over the
waterline, almost defying gravity. And then a spark of
recognition! I spot the dark-green crown of my fig tree.
Yes, I'm certain – that's it! *My* fig tree. How quickly the
tree has become *mine*.

Is it fortune or destiny that I have a direct sightline
to my tree from my thirteenth-floor apartment? It's
been right here under my nose all this time. If I hooked
up a zip-line I could whiz straight to its upper branches

in what, three minutes maybe? I start making some rough calculations, imagining where I'd secure the ropes and pulleys . . . and then my excitement flattens. The twelve-year-old in me remembers I'm trapped in a fifty-three-year-old body. *The zip-line fantasy is never going to happen.*

Just seeing my tree again makes me feel immediately nourished. I can gaze at it whenever I need. It can be my lighthouse on the headland. I feel my shoulders drop. My pulse rate slows. I notice my breathing relax.

Dr Sternberg says this soothing reaction isn't unique to me but is an example of *biophilia* at work. Biophilia is a term popularised by American biologist E.O. Wilson in the 1980s to explain our innate need to connect with the natural world. But as far back as Aristotle, thinkers and philosophers have noted our affinity with living systems and the happiness they bring us. Sunlight, fresh air, forests, flowers, birdsong, beaches – isn't that what we dream of escaping to when we're trapped in our fluorescent-lit, air-conditioned office towers? No one daydreams about pitching a tent in the middle of an expressway.

My train of thought is broken by a pair of screeching rainbow lorikeets darting past my balcony on the hunt for some lunch. A noisy miner bird is in hot pursuit. *I hope there's plenty for three.*

I wonder how my tree has survived the storm. Unlike me it had nowhere to hide or seek protection from the elements. It had to rely on its own roots to anchor it firmly in place, no matter how fierce the gale-force winds became. It had no roof from the rain. It had to shield itself with its own branches. There was no supermarket dash for toilet paper and other supplies. My tree had to rely on the soil for the nutrients it needed. Then, when the sun reappeared, its leaves continued photosynthesising, restocking its larder with carbohydrates. And all the while not only did it look after itself, but it became a refuge for other creatures – possums, birds, spiders, insects – perhaps a human or two without a bed for the night. *A community Airbnb.* My tree carried on doing all of this while I cowered in my home and put my life on hold.

When it comes to surviving, trees have got it all over us.

Back at my desk, typing all this down, a realisation flashes through my mind. Since Stargirl's death I've felt untethered and see-through, as if I would float away into space like my favourite Australian childhood television character *Mr Squiggle* . . . unable to make sense of the disconnected dots and lines on the blackboard. If Ms Jane wasn't there to hold tightly onto my green-stockinged legs, I fear I would get sucked up into the stratosphere like a lost balloon.

I want to learn how to be *more like a tree*. Strong. Resilient. Permanent. I want to know more about my tree, how it came to be where it is, and whether others feel as drawn to its aura as I do.

Tree of Life

I google the Royal Botanic Garden website, which lists someone who may hold some of the answers. Paul Nicholson has been a horticulturist at the Gardens for almost thirty years. He now runs the Gardens' volunteer and visitor programs, but it's this quote on his bio page, about why he loves his job, that intrigues me: *[I like] helping people understand that plants are central to their lives, that plants are interesting, exciting, engaging and the more time you spend with plants the happier you are likely to be.*

Sydney's shifting pandemic restrictions are still eased, so when I track Paul down I arrange to meet with him under the fig tree. When I arrive, Paul is already waiting in the dappled light, clearly curious about the unusual friendship I have struck up with one of his elderly wards.

Paul is in his early fifties and could have fallen from the pages of a children's book. Under his mop of greying, tightly bushy curls are large, expressive eyes and rosy cheeks. There's a vitality about him that only constantly being outdoors can give you. *Those cheeks are just begging to be squeezed.* I slip my hands into my pockets just in case I am tempted.

According to Paul, my Moreton Bay fig or *Ficus macrophylla* is a fine specimen with significant heritage value, probably dating back to around the 1870s. My fig tree is 150 years old! *I knew it was an old soul.*

Paul refers to his folder of copious notes. There are about 500 fig trees in the Gardens and 150 of those are Moreton Bay figs – most planted in the same era.

The Gardens' director at the time, Charles Moore, was apparently obsessed with them. He loved the generous shade they provided – although their invasive roots make them suitable for only the largest of gardens.

Mindful of not insulting a doting mother, Paul says that while my fig tree is indeed handsome, the Children's Fig Tree on the western side of Farm Cove is considered the Gardens' most prized specimen. (I later google this rival and reluctantly agree it is striking. Wider and taller than my fig and more symmetrical in form. *Not imbued with nearly as much charisma though.*)

While Moreton Bay figs are native to Queensland and New South Wales, unlike Port Jackson figs, they don't naturally occur this far south into the Sydney Basin. They're hardy stock and capable of surviving on very little.

My fig may be sturdy, but it's had some brushes with mortality. In the 1920s it survived a serious sunburning episode after it lost most of its leaves, and in the 1990s it was attacked by sap-sucking mites – fig psyllids – which thinned its bark and left it with its signature hollow. Now, its greatest threat is Mrs Macquaries Road, which pushes right up against its trunk, strangling its west-sprawling root system. How can an ugly strip of bitumen be allowed to threaten my tree? *No one falls in love with a road.*

I can see Paul is surprised by the fierce loyalty the tree has engendered in me. He's more philosophical about the tension between nature and development. Some of that is to do with his upbringing. Paul's passion for plants didn't come from his family. His father's favourite home was the one with the concreted yard – an eyesore to a nature-lover but a low-maintenance comfort for a busy dad.

As an educator, Paul is passionate about championing nature's wins. He reminds me it's still a huge blessing that New South Wales governor Lachlan Macquarie, way back in 1816, with the garden plantings having begun in 1812, set aside Sydney's Royal Botanic Garden and the Domain as areas for relaxation and scientific research. The Gardens' dramatic location, set against the city's skyscrapers, Sydney Harbour Bridge and Sydney Opera House makes it one of the most prized botanical reserves in the world.

The Gardens are Paul's domain, a grand backyard where he can immerse himself in a plant paradise. He loses himself for hours in the serpentine paths and meandering dips and rises, flowering gums around one bend and then a dense copse of palms in the shadows up ahead. This is a genteel wildness that doesn't scare or intimidate.

It was a sacred site for Indigenous tribes, an initiation site or *bora ground*, and now it's a spiritual meeting place for modern-day Sydneysiders. Even though there are more than 25,000 plants on these 30 hectares, it's the tree elders – like mine – that link the past to the present. *They are the time travellers.*

My tree has seen so much life. It has seen so much death.

From its vantage point on the hill, my tree has watched as men intoxicated with gold fever spilled out of boats at the Woolloomooloo docks in the mid-1800s and strode off inland to the goldfields to make their fortune or meet their folly; during the First World War my tree would have looked on from the hill with a heavy heart as thousands of young men set sail from the same wharves to the Western Front, full of hope and adventure, many never to return, the others, broken men with no words for the horror they had witnessed; and in 1918–19 my tree would have seen the deep human scars left by that last devastating pandemic – the Spanish flu.

Through it all it would have sheltered others like me, the wounded and broken. It would have been – as it is now – a place of solace and safety. It couldn't fix, it couldn't change. All it could do was be present. *The greatest comfort anyone can offer.*

Paul tells me it's not encouraged, but many people bring the ashes of their loved ones to scatter through the Gardens. The Rose Garden, with its pink and red-velvet blooms, is particularly popular. The begonia beds bursting with sunset hues is another favourite. I can see there would be few more beautiful resting places.

Several days later I'm back to visit my tree and find that someone has placed a small brown ceramic urn in one of its hollows. There's a pang in my heart. Another departed soul who also felt the specialness of this place. I sit with them for a long time, thinking of them visiting this tree, imagining the life they would have lived and those they have left behind – maybe a loved one torn apart like me.

The ripples from a death touch so many. Close family and friends and then the friends and family of those family and friends. It can create a village of grief. Although to be missed isn't a comfort bestowed on everyone. I've seen at the Wayside Chapel, the homeless crisis centre in Kings Cross where I am an ambassador, that many people get forgotten long before they die.

So here I am, sitting with this friend of my tree, their earthly remains encased in this urn – reduced to a container of powdery ash and dust – but where is their essence? Dancing with the stars perhaps? Maybe Stargirl is with them, dazzling as always, taking the new arrival under her angel wings. The two of them zipping through the Milky Way, joyous and sparkling, finding new loves, touching more hearts.

As if to prove how fleeting the physical can be, when I return the next morning, the urn – like Stargirl – is gone.

The sands of time have come to collect another.

CHAPTER 7

Cricket

When we were growing up, I always felt my parents were searching for something that didn't really exist. Perpetual excitement, freedom, acceptance? Whatever it was, it seemed to hover just out of their reach. It made for an adventurous childhood.

By the time I was thirteen we had lived in five countries – South Africa, Zambia, England, Australia, Zimbabwe and then back to Australia. My father, a cricket tragic, would often joke that he would only settle his family in countries as obsessed with cricket as he was. If Australia didn't work out, we feared we'd be heading across the ditch to New Zealand next. Don't get me wrong, we loved our *fush and chups*. But the only notable New Zealand cricketers at the time were Richard Hadlee and the Crowe brothers. *How could we be expected to swear allegiance to a country with a second-rate cricket team?*

Stargirl, Dreamcatcher and I were blooded in the sport as infants. The thwack of leather on willow became the soundtrack of our summers. The thundering run-up from Jeff Thompson; the acrobatic dives in the outfield; the grass stains on crisp whites; the zinc cream, tinnies and sombreros; the roar from the crowd . . . *Howzat!*

Cricket commentators Tony Greig, Richie Benaud and Bill Lawry were the Holy Trinity, their reassuring voices streaming out of the telly, able to calm and excite like Sunday evangelists. Household chores and activities would be timed around Tony Greig's morning assessment of the playing pitch. Wearing his trademark cream panama hat, Tony would fold his lanky length into a crouch on the pitch and poke a car key or a pen into a grassy crack, the camera going in for a dramatic close-up. We'd hold our breath waiting for his verdict. If the crack was moist, the pitch would favour the bowlers; hard and dry and it could be a good day for the batting side.

Inexplicably, and proving how impressionable young children can be, we would then run around the backyard playing *pitch report*, plunging mum's house key into the garden until it was caked with mud and it was time for the lunch session to begin.

Unsurprisingly, the town of Launceston in northern Tasmania, where we lived at the time, didn't feature prominently on the tour schedules of visiting international cricket teams.

Cricket

One summer, though, the all-star West Indies team is in town for an exhibition match against the Tasmanian state side. The three of us are beside ourselves. Viv Richards, Gus Logie, Clive Lloyd right here in our home town!

As usual, we three girls plan our day at the cricket. No need for Mum and Dad, who will be at work. Our preparations begin in the early hours of match day. Cricketing accoutrements are retrieved from the hall cupboard – picnic basket, thermos, cushions, wide-brimmed hats, binoculars, a transistor radio and our autograph books. Chicken luncheon-slice sandwiches are wrapped and chilled, hot sweet tea is brewed with a dash of condensed milk. As we set off with our members' tickets securely in our pockets, we look more like nerdy retirees than pre-teen fangirls.

We arrive at the ground's turnstiles hours before the start of play. It's overcast, with glints of sunshine breaking through the banks of cloud. Dozens of families are streaming in through the gates, armed with esky coolers and green and gold flags. We may be *members*, but the seat allocation in the Members' area is still egalitarian: first come, first served. We're in luck! We snare a green wooden bench high in the stands, in the shade, next to the concrete steps that lead to the players' changerooms. This is a prized position. We've seen this on television. If you time your advance perfectly, you may be able to give a congratulatory slap or tap to the back of one of your favourite players as he jogs past. A chance for a mere mortal to touch a god.

We must be such a curiosity to the local cricketing fraternity – three dark-skinned little girls, on their own, in the mainly white, male Members' Stand, setting themselves up for a day of cricket when most of their schoolfriends are at the cinema watching *Herbie Goes Bananas*. We've never been much in step with our peer group.

There's an announcement on the speakers. The West Indies have won the toss and elected to bowl. The crowd stands in anticipation as West Indies fast bowler Michael Holding sprints in for the first ball of the day. It's a bouncer that beats opening batsman and local hero David Boon. There's a collective *Ooooh!* from the crowd. Even the wicketkeeper's heroic dive can't stop this missile. It races all the way to the boundary fence for four runs. There's a cheer and we settle back into our seats. The West Indies may be black and glamorous, but we still want the Aussies to crush them.

It's the end of the over. Stargirl is restless. She's heading to the fence line to see if she can snare an autograph from one of the West Indies boundary fielders. An excited gaggle of kids has already gathered down there, waving their autograph books, hoping for a signature they can brag about at Show and Tell on Monday.

Stargirl runs down the concrete steps, eyes shining with the thrill of the chase. She's soon swallowed up by the throng of little people. Dreamcatcher and I keep half an eye on her as she valiantly attempts to get a fielder's attention. She's so tiny though. Her little arms can barely reach over the white picket fence.

The crowd is on its feet again. Michael Holding runs in for another delivery. *Bam!* The ball hits middle stump, sending a bail spinning into the air. Boon is out! One for 56 rolls onto the huge black scoreboard on the hill. The first wicket has fallen just before the morning-tea break.

The drinks cart, sporting a yellow-and-orange-striped umbrella, is wheeled through the gate onto the field. The new batsman high-fives a despondent Boonie as they pass each other on the stairs. Back in the middle of the field the scenes are jubilant. The Windies have twisted into a human knot, celebrating their prized wicket, their smiles blinding white against their dark skin.

I scan the group of kids near the fence, looking for Stargirl. She's sitting down on a bench, with the auto-graph hunters now focusing their attention on *her* not the fielders. A small boy breaks away from the scrum and runs back up the steps past me waving his autograph book in the air. *Mum! Dad! Look at the autograph I got!*

I'm filled with foreboding. *This better not be what I think it is.* I run down the stairs and push my way through the crush of kids to find Stargirl scribbling in an autograph book. I move in closer to see what she is writing. *Manika Richards.*

Horrified, I yank her away by the arm and demand to know what she is doing. She tells me that one of the kids has asked her – because she is black – if she is related to a West Indies player. Not thinking about the ramifications of her fib, Stargirl has said, *Yes, Vivian Richards is my dad.* The *daughter* of a West Indian cricketer is celebrity enough for these country kids, and before Stargirl can wriggle out of the hole she has dug for herself she is swooped upon by autograph hunters.

I'm mortified by her deception. I tell her she is going to be in *so* much trouble with Mum and Dad when we get home. I can see even she is amazed by her own naughtiness. I never do tell my parents though. I figure – how often is just *being black* going to make you a celebrity in Australia? Everyone does eventually hear about the autograph scam when I share the memory as part of my eulogy at Stargirl's funeral. For the briefest of moments sad smiles flicker on the distraught faces.

Later I think about her made-up signature still adorning those autograph books. Those children would now be grown-ups, possibly still cherishing her name on their pages, their books safely stowed away in a dusty box on a garage shelf. To them it's a keepsake of a special day in their childhoods. A day when *they* were left feeling special.

Maybe Stargirl didn't do such a bad thing after all.

CHAPTER 8

Birds of a Feather

There's a feathery stroke against my cheek. I drowsily open my eyes but my husband Mark is still asleep. I roll over and look out onto the balcony. The caress I felt is from a dawn breeze through the curtains, so whisper-soft it could have been the sigh of nature itself. It leaves my skin tingling, nerve-endings along my back, shoulders and collarbone igniting with pinpricks of arousal.

I'm being tempted out of hibernation.

These sensations are my first tentative steps towards reinhabiting my body. I'm unfurling like a new flower bud, slowly rediscovering my veins and arteries, muscles and limbs, willing the life force to return. This is a battle the Jedi warrior in me must win. I'm hoping Yoda's wise voice will guide me back to my lightsaber, guide me back to where I lost it on that cold night in May, the night I lost Stargirl. *Do or Do Not. There is no Try.*

Numbness serves an important role when you're first electrocuted by the shock of grief. It's the trip-switch that prevents your entire grid from overloading and short-circuiting. It allows your autonomic system to function, independent of your emotional shutdown – breathing, digestion, cell renewal all tick over like clockwork even though there's no driver behind the wheel. It's remarkable how little of *us* our bodies actually need to stay alive.

While your body becomes the paramedic, your mind becomes the neurosurgeon, trying to reassemble its shattered fragments, pieces of broken eggshell so numerous and indistinguishable, it seems an exercise in madness. You recall the childhood nursery rhyme you recited all those years ago . . . *All the king's horses and all the king's men couldn't put Humpty together again.*

I just want to feel safe. Instead, I have the hyper-vigilance of a hunted animal, perpetually frozen on my haunches, ears cocked, nose sniffing the breeze, primed for another attack. Something as mundane as popping down to the supermarket for some milk is like entering an underground interrogation chamber: refrigerated air as cold as a morgue, blinding overhead lights, torturous cheery voices assailing me from loudspeakers, the clanging of metal trolleys, masked faces with furtive eyes.

Disorientated in this maze of aisles, I have a flash of clarity. When I take my walk and I'm with my tree, there are no disturbing sounds or sudden visual jolts.

No drilling or droning, grinding or grating. Time passes in soothing waves of serenity. The light is filtered, sounds are subdued: the tranquillity of *green silence* pervades everything, as British nature writer Robert Macfarlane so perfectly describes it. Even though my tree is also subjected to this constant tremor of suburban disharmony, it manages to maintain its equilibrium, radiating an unflappable calm – unlike my broken parts, which would spill out of me if my skin didn't hold them together.

I need to see my fig tree again. The shopping will have to be abandoned.

I shuffle my morning plans around so I can drop by for a visit. It will tie in nicely with the catch-up I've organised in the Royal Botanic Garden with my next urban spirit guide – a scientist who has made one of nature's most ethereal creations part of her life's work.

There's an invigorating crispness in the air as I set out along Macleay Street and join the commuter throng in suits and sneakers, treading the same short cut through the Botanic Garden to the CBD. The tight clamp across my ribs has eased, my breathing is steadying, the caged bird inside me can finally spread its wings.

Summer is lazily unwinding into autumn. Piles of papery brown leaves from the plane trees carpet the pavement, crunching deliciously underfoot. There's so much to rejoice in these leaves: their colours, form and sound. The way they pirouette in the wind with such playfulness and vitality it's almost impossible to view them as no longer alive. But that is technically what they are. *Departed. Expired. Deceased.* Watching them reminds me of the Monty Python 'Dead Parrot' sketch ... remember that classic gem? Customer Mr Praline, played by John Cleese, becomes more and more exasperated with the pet shop owner, played by Michael Palin, who refuses to acknowledge he has sold him a dead parrot.

Mr Praline: 'E's 'opped the twig! 'E's kicked the bucket, 'e's shuffled off 'is mortal coil, run down the curtain and joined the bleedin' choir invisible! THIS IS AN EX-PARROT!

(I had the pleasure of listening to this brilliant sketch again, when I interviewed the very 'alive and kicking' John Cleese on my radio show about his book *Creativity*.)

The parrot and the leaves may be dead, but I'm beginning to understand more deeply the naturalness in their passing. They'll decompose and nourish more life. The branches of the plane trees above me will soon be sprouting new green shoots, eager to take their place in the continuum.

The army of commuters trudging alongside me seems oblivious to these quiet miracles. While we're lost in our heads or in our devices, nature's cycle of renewal rolls on quietly in the background despite our distraction. Eventually everything must return to the earth. I'm seeing that more clearly now. Death doesn't have to be a rip in the universe.

It's something reinforced in the insightful writings of English psychiatrist and psychotherapist Sue Stuart-Smith. Her book *The Well Gardened Mind* is bobbing along in my canvas shoulder bag as I stride down the McElhone Stairs, glimpses of Woolloomooloo Bay poking through the cascades of lantana. Sue Stuart-Smith's clinical work with death and depression keeps her largely indoors, which was why, she writes, she was drawn to gardening and the outdoors for some solace. Being in nature reminds her of the continuity of life and how our day-to-day lives are part of the cycle of death. But she warns: *If we think about dying too much it interferes with living, but if we never think about death, we remain perilously unprepared.*

Urban nature is constantly giving us clues to this life-and-death cycle with the ephemera it scatters across our path. It's not only trees and plants that shed parts of themselves. Birds are discarding their plumage constantly. On a recent walk to my tree, I stumbled upon a mass of white downy cockatoo feathers on the hill, so many in number, it looked like the scene of an exuberant pillow fight during a slumber party.

Since that discovery I can't help but see feathers everywhere during my morning strolls: immaculate, long, glossy tail feathers – which could easily adorn a fashionista's hat at the Melbourne Cup – strewn through a grevillea bed; small puffs of breast feathers caught in the thorns of an acacia bush; wing feathers – bent and salt-encrusted – discarded on the pavement; and manky ones, covered in grime and bird poo, lying forlornly in the gutter.

Who were the owners of all these feathers and do they miss their prized plumage? Are they missed the way I pine for Stargirl? Perhaps the *feathers* are the ones doing the mourning? Doesn't the fragment always grieve for its whole?

Few people know more about feathers and their provenance than Kate Brandis, whom I'm on my way to meet. When I interviewed Kate on my radio show, I was impressed by her dedication and insight. I want to understand a bird's connection to its feathers, so Kate is joining me on a feather-hunting expedition near my tree.

Kate arrives at the entrance to the Andrew (Boy) Charlton Pool for our treasure hunt almost bird-like herself – noiseless, bright-eyed and attentive. She's dressed in grey sneakers, an olive-green puffer vest and jeans, perfectly camouflaged with our surrounds.

We set off up the slope through a stand of flowering gum trees, eyes peering intently at the ground. A life spent in intimate proximity to birds imbues Kate with an avian dimension. While I stomp across the landscape, she skips lightly like a sparrow; where my movements are rough and sudden, hers are lithe and graceful; while I fidget, she remains deeply present. As a salty harbour gust moves through the eucalypts above us, I notice how every one of Kate's senses is ignited by the encounter. This is what being fully alive should look like. I now have a template to emulate.

Birds of a Feather

Kate's brown eyes pool with sympathy when I mention Stargirl's death and my quest to find solace in nature. I share with her Stargirl's love of bushwalks and camping, and her affinity with water. Kate drops her eyes and tilts her head in silence, and I suddenly feel a gaping sorrow as I'm haunted again by that recurring question – *Why wasn't the incandescent wonder of all this enough for Stargirl?*

Recent heavy downpours have washed away much of the surface litter, so we don't see any feathers for several metres. But after a few minutes Kate spies our first specimen. It's from an ibis. A long tail feather, as pristine white as fresh snow, with a brown velvety tip. It would make an excellent quill pen. Kate explains that ibis shed feathers from their wings and tails once a year. When a feather gets tattered and frayed it loses its aerodynamic strength and needs to be replaced by a new one. Inspecting this feather, my amateur eye can't find a fault. It's perfect. Soft and glossy, each barb on each wisp hooking onto the next in a gentle curve, like fine teeth on an elegant comb. The spine of the feather is immaculate as well – a thin, tapering, see-through straw of papery resin. Why would this feather have been discarded? Kate says it may have been dislodged during a fight or accident or during an amorous encounter. She explains that birds feel no pain when they lose their feathers, but when a key tail or wing feather attached to a nerve dislodges, birds do feel a little discomfort – similar to what a cat may feel if you pulled off one of its whiskers. *Ouch!* I pop this feather in my bag. It's a keeper.

I was fascinated by feathers as a child. They were so soft to touch. I loved their shape and colours, and how they quivered when you blew on them gently. I kept a feather collection in a shoebox under my bed and would add to it weekly during walks to school or on holiday weekends when we went beachcombing. My prize feather was too big for my box and sat in a jar on my desk. It was a dazzling peacock plume I spotted during a school hike through Cataract Gorge in Launceston. The peacocks had been imported to the Gorge reserve to attract more visitors – an incongruous idea but a successful one, as crowds would often gather to watch these regal immigrants sashay among the muted-toned wallabies and gum trees.

Kate and I make our way down the hilly slope towards Mrs Macquaries Point, navigating muddy puddles as we go. My mood lifts as my fig tree appears over the rise and I excitedly point it out to Kate. She stops and murmurs appreciatively, inspecting my colossal friend as a bird would, taking in its wide, safe branches, hidden hollows and plentiful supply of new fruit.

We find more feathers here. Soft downy cockatoo feathers, some with a blush of yellow, and a few tiny grey ones that could belong to the pair of figbirds I've watched honeymooning in my tree's lower branches. If we didn't collect these feathers, other creatures would repurpose them. Other birds will use them to insulate their nests.

Birds of a Feather

Kate reminds me that even the catacomb of rodent nests under the city would be lined with downy feathers.

I first encountered Kate, who is a university researcher with a PhD, no less, when she was heading a fascinating project mapping the movements of Australia's waterbirds by tracking their fallen feathers. This endeavour captured the imagination of citizen scientists across the country, and hundreds of envelopes of feathers began arriving at Kate's laboratory at the University of New South Wales in Sydney. Big ones, little ones, long ones, fat ones, white and cream, black and brown, glossy and mottled. Enough feathers to fill several doonas in fact!

Kate used the feathers to create the country's first 'feather map'. By scanning each feather and measuring its potassium, calcium and sodium levels, Kate was able to pinpoint where the birds were geographically when each feather was grown.

Her results were astonishing. Kate found that 60 per cent of the feathers collected were grown in the Murray–Darling River Basin, proving how critical this fragile basin area – stretching from Queensland in the north to New South Wales and Victoria in the south – is for bird survival. Saving these precious breeding grounds suddenly feels more pressing than ever.

The feathers I collected as a child gave me so much joy; looking back now, I wonder why I stopped delighting in them. Kate suggests my disconnection from feathers may have been partly to do with simply growing taller.

When you're a child you're closer to the ground. You notice what's around your feet – feathers, or shells on the beach, shiny pebbles, lichen-covered sticks, tiny ants. Their world is your world. Children are more conscious of being *in* the earth not just *on* it. They develop a *topophilia* or place-love for these treasured spaces. They do handstands, build caves and castles, roll around and daydream in it. They develop an intimacy with these earth places that the adults in their world eventually pull them away from by insisting that they *Don't put things in your mouth*, or *Always wear shoes* or *Don't walk on the grass*. Eventually the calling cards of nature – like feathers – become something removed, foreign and dirty.

Rather than seeing feathers, as we once did, as magic wands capable of transporting us to wondrous places, we treat them with the cruellest of disregard. *We stop seeing them.* We grind them underfoot into the pavement. They become little more than detritus, these glorious sculptures of keratin that enable birds to ride the winds in any direction while keeping them warm and dry and protected. Spending the morning gathering these talismans of nature makes me realise how much more resilient one of these feathery puffs is than how I feel right now. How can I unlock their secret, the way they transform their vulnerable sensuousness into a coat of armour?

Maybe that's what a feather can teach me. That my fragility *is* my strength. Perhaps I shouldn't see the fractures and losses as weaknesses: the chinks in my breastplate are just the scars of the battles I've weathered and survived. I share this thought with Kate.

She smiles with her bird-brown eyes and nods, adding that a feather represents multiples of strength. The individual filament on a feather is strong but not as strong as the many filaments that combine to form the feather. A feather is durable but not as robust as a wing. And a bird is spirited but not as invincible as a flock. Strength comes from the resilience of the smallest link in the chain.

My own chain of three is now broken. One of the links severed from the collective. Can the two remaining links – Dreamcatcher and I – still be a chain? Or will the metal fatigue caused by Stargirl's death eventually erode our links as well?

That's why feathers on your path are like totems, says Kate. *They are the end of things and the sign of new beginnings.*

CHAPTER 9
Highland Dancing

It's 1977. The house is awash with tartan. It's the highland dancing state finals this weekend. Nerves are frayed, mouths are pouting, feet are being stomped. Even the cat can sense the frisson of tension as her persistent purrs for attention go unnoticed.

Here in Tasmania, where the snowy peaks and wintery weather mimic the Scottish Uplands, highland dancing has taken a bizarre cultural foothold. It's a serious pursuit with highly medalled competitors achieving god-like status. At school it's offered as an extracurricular activity, with those showing promise fast-tracked into various dance academies.

My elephant feet have hampered my attempts at glory, but Dreamcatcher and Stargirl have joined the hallowed ranks of the gifted few. If two dark-skinned Indian South African girls standing on the winners' podium, in their tartan skirts and bonnets, causes a double take in Tasmania in the 1970s, no one mentions it to us.

Stargirl and Dreamcatcher are obsessed. They practise incessantly. *Toe and heel and toe and heel.* Building their strength so one leg can take their body weight while the other leg can point and extend and tap the floor. They spend hours flicking through costume books, fantasising about their outfits for their various dance routines. Among the repertoire they need to perfect are the Jig, the Reel, the Highland Fling and of course the dramatic Sword Dance. The dress code is exacting. Each dance demands a different costume. The judges mark you on your attire as well as how well you execute the various dance manoeuvres.

The mail-out list of dos and don'ts is enough to give any parent a conniption:

* *Highland slippers compulsory.*

* *No jewellery is to be worn.*

* *No nail polish.*

* *No headbands or decorative clips (plain bobby pins and a hairnet are required).*

* *Hair should be tied back neatly off the face – bun or French braid.*

(PLEASE HAVE MISS EMMETT SEE THE ENTIRE OUTFIT PRIOR TO THE COMPETITION.)

Highland Dancing

* *Bring lots of safety pins to the competition.*

* *Bring bobby pins, hairnet, hairspray, lipstick (optional) and comb.*

* *Highland Kilt Outfit (worn for Pas de Basques, High-cuts and highland dances such as Fling, Sword, and Reel).*

* *White knee socks (or tartan socks to match the same tartan in the kilt).*

* *Elastics at the top of the socks to prevent the socks from falling down.*

* *Black underpants under kilt.*

* *Kilt or kiltie (the kiltie has less material and is great for primary or beginner dancers).*

* *White highland blouse.*

* *Highland vest over blouse or highland jacket with lace dickey (optional).*

* *White Dress or Aboyne (worn for Lilt, Flora and other national dances).*

* *White petticoat for under dress.*

* *White underpants under dress.*

* *White ankle socks (white knee socks acceptable for young dancers).*

The industry created around the vast wardrobe required for these competitions is reputed to keep the Scottish economy afloat. *A bobby-pin-led recovery.*

Most of these dance outfits are custom-made. It's an expense that a family with three competing dancers can ill afford, so the hunt is always on for second-hand or recycled bargains. Stargirl is not happy about this. As the youngest in a family of three girls she has always refused hand-me-downs. Her clothes are her expression, her armour. She has an innate sense of style. Even as a nine-year-old she dresses immaculately. Unlike me, she never pulls anything off the dirty-clothes pile on the floor.

She was born a diva.

Keeping up with the financial costs of highland dancing competitions brings out our parents' ingenuity. Mum's handy sewing skills are put to good use. Skirts, blouses and aprons are expertly whipped up on her trusty Janome sewing machine. And Dad disappears into the garage workshop and emerges at the end of the weekend with timber offcuts transformed into swashbuckling swords for Sword Dance practice. Sadly, we are unappreciative of their extraordinary efforts and fear the judges will mark us down because our costumes are handmade. (Writing this I wish I could go back and apologise for us being ungrateful little brats.)

Since I've failed to make the finals, I'm relegated to chief bag-carrier and wardrobe assistant. Coat bags are arranged on the kitchen table, with each outfit laid out from socks to hairnets. As Mum goes through a final inspection before we pile into the car, she notices that the lace cap needed for Stargirl's Lilt dance is missing. It was my job to borrow one from a schoolfriend but I have forgotten. Missing a head cover could mean point deductions or even disqualification. *I'll never hear the end of it.* Terrified of admitting I've stuffed up, I tell Mum I have it in my bag and all will be fine. As the tartan entourage heads for the car, I make a dash to the living room to gather something I'm certain will make a pretty good replacement for the lace cap. I tell no one.

A makeshift wooden stage has been erected at the showgrounds. A bracing wind is cutting through the bleachers where all the parents and competitors are finding their seats. The oak trees rustle against the tin roof. The dancers, in their warm woollen outfits, are the only ones who are dressed for the conditions.

The first age group heads to the marshalling area near the stage. Competition numbers are pinned to their waistcoats, hair is tidied, kilts are straightened, shoe ribbons are tucked in and socks are pulled up high just below the knee. A music tape is dropped into the cassette player and the competition kicks into action. A few of the dancers miss their opening cue and get flustered as they try to fall back in step. They're back in time. Disaster averted. Perfectly arched arms, supporting leg turned out at the hip and extended toe points. They look like perfect music-box dancers.

Dreamcatcher is next on stage and blitzes the field with her elegant stance and perfect rhythm. The last challenge is the trickiest. She prepares for the Sword Dance, an ancient dance of war that dates back to the 1700s. Highland warriors celebrated their victories by dancing over two crossed swords. As well as showing off their superior fitness and talent, dancing without touching the swords was seen as a good omen for battles ahead. Dancing without touching the swords? Frightening for some, exhilarating for others.

In competitions, several marks are lost if you touch the swords. *This may explain why the Sword Dance was never a strong element in Stargirl's repertoire. She has always been fascinated by the edges of things.* In contrast, the Sword Dance is Dreamcatcher's forte. She is wary of boundaries and edges and has learned to tread carefully. She's the middle one. Always hemmed in. Flanked on either side by us. Trapped and protected from the edges. Until now. *I still have a younger sister. She does not. Now she is the edge.*

This seismic shift of sororal geography is still decades into the future. Right now, the only edges Dreamcatcher is focused on are the ones on these swords. I can see her channel her highland ancestors (*ha ha*) as the blades are carried into the arena and arranged reverentially on the stage. The crowd goes quiet as all eyes focus on Dreamcatcher's leather slippers and the glinting edge of the swords. As the bagpipes sound she leaps up, then in and over the swords, twirling in perfect pirouettes. Her performance is flawless and she beams when she hears her high score.

Next is the Fling, another dance of battle – and another test of strength and agility. The dance is said to mimic deer bounding across the heather; others say the dancer's upturned arms represent the antlers of stags at play. Dream-catcher's eyes are steely and determined. She summons the highland gods and is again among the medallists.

Stargirl's dance category is next – the Lilt. She looks picture perfect in her red cotton frock floating on layers of flouncing white petticoats. All she is missing is her lace bonnet. As mothers swoop in to fuss over their daughters for the final touches, I race up to Stargirl at the very last moment and, without her noticing, affix my makeshift lace cap to her hair just as she's stepping onto the stage. I'm certain no one will ever guess its provenance.

As Stargirl's group begins its dance there are raised eyebrows from the judges and stifled giggles ripple through the bleachers. Stargirl is distracted by the murmurs and looks around, losing her concentration for a moment. Somehow, she refocuses as the chuckles now become audible laughter. I start sinking into my parka as I realise what they are laughing at.

Look at that little Indian girl! Is that a doily she's wearing on her head? Mum, who's been repairing a loose button on a costume, looks up to see what all the commotion is about. Her eyes widen and she shoots me one of her withering *if looks could kill* looks.

Stargirl finishes her dance and pulls her cap off to discover it is a doily from one of the headrests on our sofa at home. Her furious eyes find me in the crowd and she stomps off the stage, heading in my direction. *Hell hath no fury like a highland dancer doilied!* It will be days before she talks to me again. I am a pariah in the family, forced to walk to class alone and banished after school to watch TV on my own in the kitchen.

I don't know what all the fuss was about. She still got a silver medal.

CHAPTER 10

On a Wing and a Prayer

Gggggrrrrreeeekkk! The unmistakable screech of tiny claws on metal.

I look up from my keyboard to see a flapping pied currawong clinging to the railing of my balcony for dear life. He's misjudged his landing speed and has had to hit the brakes hard, skidding like an out-of-control 747. He regains his balance almost immediately though, as if it's all been part of a *Disney on Ice* circus spectacular, effortlessly swinging his body back upright, ruffled black feathers smooth and streamlined again, head tilted, poised for any danger. *Nothing to see here.*

He hasn't fooled me. I can see the heart palpitations behind his breast feathers, as the blood swooshes to his wingtips. *That was a close call.* When he sees me through my office window, his body suddenly contracts with fear.

To him I am a predator like the rest of my kind. It hurts that I could be prejudged this way. But he knows what I'm capable of, better than I do.

For a fraction of a second our eyes meet. Mine wounded and vulnerable, his amber and defiant. Do I detect in that piercing look a hint of humiliation that his less than agile touchdown has been observed? I put on my best sympathetic face but he won't have a bar of it, abruptly turning his glossy tail feathers to me and pretending to intently scan the neighbourhood for some breakfast. A car horn sounds below and my visitor takes his cue. He transforms his body into an aerodynamic wetsuit of feathers, and spear-dives over a row of penthouses towards Elizabeth Bay, his earlier lumbering landing clearly an anomaly.

Nearby, another currawong's call breaks through the rising cacophony of jackhammering and garbage trucks. *Kio-kio wheeo, kio-kio wheeo.* There's so much grace and gratitude in those lilting notes. I imagine he's saying: *Hey everyone, I made it through the night. Death didn't come for me. I get a bonus day.* And you just know he's not going to waste it. No hurried morning commute for him, crammed into a train compartment so he can sit under fluorescent lights in a hermetically sealed airless office. *No, no, no.*

I imagine his day will be pure freedom, flitting from tree to tree – dropping in for the occasional balcony visit – chasing after some breakfast, maybe a butterfly or two, or plundering the berries on a backyard fruit tree. Then a visit to the neighbourhood watering holes, perhaps a splash in Kings Cross's iconic El Alamein Fountain, or if those pesky white ibis are hogging the best spots, maybe that warm puddle that collects in the bush rock in the Arthur McElhone Reserve gardens. After a refreshing dip, another circuit of the Domain and then maybe a chinwag with the boys on the rooftop aerial of the Macleay Regis apartment block. You can get a serious jazz sway happening if enough mates can be rallied. All in all, not a bad way to spend a day in the hood. *Birds understand instinctively that* now *is all we ever really have.*

From the west, an acrid smoke haze is blowing in over the Sydney Basin. Another ill-timed hazard-reduction burn in preparation for bushfire season. It mingles with the light and scatters a dusty rose glow across the clouds, turning them into puffs of ashen fairy floss. I picture myself, like the currawong, catching a breeze, my wingtips slicing through the edge of those clouds, dipping and soaring with the thermals, then gliding down to my tree and cocooning in its branches. *A biped's bird envy.*

My feather hunting with Kate Brandis has deepened my interest in my neighbourhood birds – particularly the ones that roost in my tree. As well as the figbirds, I've noticed regular visits from rainbow lorikeets, magpies, noisy miners, white-necked herons, and even a tawny frogmouth or two. And they're just the species my untrained eye can identify. A host of others dart in and out, grazing on the fig berries, collecting materials for their nest-building or stealing some respite from the weather.

Their comings and goings fascinate me even though I'm not a natural *watcher*. Before Stargirl's death froze me in my tracks, I'd been too busy *doing* to be fully aware of the tiny moments of wonder unfurling around me. Tree-time is changing that. As soon as I step into my tree's shadow, a cloak of stillness slips over me. It's like sleeping fully awake. There's a hypnotising tranquillity under its green chandelier. The stillness becomes its own radiance. Birdwatchers have turned being still into an art form. It's the state required to truly understand a bird's habits and habitat.

As I return to my tree again and again, its feathery visitors and their routines are becoming more familiar the stiller I become. I notice how some are entwined in pairs while others are loners; how size has no bearing on aggression – the tiniest are sometimes the most pugilistic; how the rainbow lorikeets are the chattering clowns; and how, when the sulphur-crested cockatoos come marauding through, everyone else makes themselves scarce.

There's actually a birdwatching term for returning to the same place again and again to identify and study the birds in the area. It's known as *atlassing* – and in a way, I imagine, my regular visits to my tree have been a form of atlassing. I'm discovering that the world of bird-watching is a mysterious one. The terminology alone can be bewildering.

I'm apparently a *dude* – a birdwatcher who doesn't know that much about birds. A *stringer* is someone who incorrectly records sightings of birds. (This could be me as well.) And a *twitcher* is a birdwatcher prepared to travel great distances to see a rare bird and cross it off their bucket list. Twitchers – to the serious birdwatcher – are to be derided. To *dip* is to miss out on seeing a bird you are looking for. And to *grip* is to see a bird another birder has missed and to tell them you've seen it. (This sounds more like *gloating* to me.)

I realise I need assistance navigating this birdwatching minefield, so I ring someone who surprises many with his knowledge of birds – my dear friend and fellow broadcaster, comedian Steve Abbott. He is a wise owl in our friendship network and I am really looking forward to his enjoyable company.

Steve is best known to millions of Australians as his alter ego, comedian The Sandman – the man-child with a penchant for taking off his clothes in public. What many of his fans probably don't know, is that Steve has been enamoured of birds for more than twenty years. In fact, he says it was birdwatching that saved him when his marriage and career simultaneously imploded, leaving him bankrupt and homeless. He didn't share this with me at the time, so I'm deeply intrigued to learn how the simple act of watching birds could soften the blow of two life-changing calamities. I ask him if he can join me at the Royal Botanic Garden one morning later in the week and he says he would love to.

As I bound up the Woolloomooloo marina stairs to meet Steve, patches of blue sky begin poking through the smoke shroud. Here and there, sunshine dances on the harbour in golden hues so pure and perfect it stops my heart. This is what Ralph Waldo Emerson called the *perfect exhilaration*. Why weren't days like these enough for Stargirl? Why couldn't whatever anguish she carried deep within her soul be doused by the glorious balm of a day like this? And then the most unsettling doubt bubbles just below the surface . . . *if the fingers of darkness could come for her, could they come for me?*

I pass a young couple leaving the (Boy) Charlton Pool with wet, tangled hair, their cheeks flushed from an invigorating morning dip. Just behind them is Steve, perched on the hill, in a cuddly grey pullover, warm and woolly like a week-old kookaburra. (As I'm writing this passage something incredible happens. It's just before sunbreak. Grey wispy clouds are trailing low in the purple sky when a young kookaburra lands on the balcony railing right in front of my desk! He appears precisely as I'm typing the word K.O.O.K.A.B.U.R.R.A. on my keypad. Have I conjured up a spirit guide just by willing it? I'm flabbergasted by the coincidence. This little kooka is a beauty. He gives me a full stare. No fear here. His speckled brown tail feathers quiver slightly as he steadies himself in the breeze. The caramel down on his chest is as delicate as a dandelion. And his eyes, deep and knowing, are filled with such kindness. Before I can get my breath back, he swivels round, gives me one last look over his shoulder, and, with a whoosh of his wings, flaps off into the day. It happens so quickly I'm not entirely sure if I imagined it. What makes this encounter even more extraordinary is that it's the first time I've ever seen a kookaburra on my balcony. It puts a smile on my face for the rest of the morning.)

Back at the Royal Botanic Garden, Steve greets me with a fortifying hug, his large brown eyes smiling, ready to play. He looks just as I remember: wavy, greying hair with spiky whiskers. A little frayed around the edges. My mood lifts immediately. Over the years we've made numerous television and radio shows together, but what we've done most is make each other laugh.

We fall into an easy chatter as we head along Mrs Macquaries Road to the fig tree, where two patrol cars of Federal Police officers are enjoying a coffee break. Even though they're relaxed and sharing some jokes, I'm rattled to see men with guns – and the implied violence of them – this close to my tree.

I spread a picnic rug and some pillows under a eucalypt across the road. We talk about Stargirl and how I am coping. I tell him I expected I would have good days and bad days but I didn't expect to have good hours and bad hours *within the same morning*. The emotional swings are exhausting. Steve shares stories of his own grief when his mother died, and reassures me that the old cliché that time heals is indeed true but the wait can be agonising.

We settle in for a few hours of watching. Steve wants to remind me that he's only an amateur birder and most of what he can teach me he has learned from the Australian birdwatching bible *What Bird Is That?*. Neville Cayley wrote and illustrated this authoritative field guide in 1935, and it's rarely been out of print. It's recently been updated to include all of Australia's 830 bird species – twenty of which call Sydney's Royal Botanic Garden home.

It's time to ask Steven the big question: is it required for birdwatchers to wear their pants pulled up high under their armpits? *Are all birders Harry-high-pants?* Steve lets this gentle ribbing roll, like water off a duck's back. He says that while most birdwatchers do indeed tend to be older retirees, the only qualification required to be a successful birdwatcher is to be a good *watcher*. It's essentially the art of making yourself small and insignificant. Steve says he discovered – the hard way – the important life lessons that can flow from this state.

Twenty years ago, Steve's marriage ended when he met someone else. He says it precipitated a *perfect storm*. The emotional upheaval coincided with a crossroads in his television career, and before he knew it, he was homeless. While juggling the passion of a new love with the dying embers of an old one, his life spiralled out of control.

In the middle of this maelstrom, a friend gave him a copy of *What Bird Is That?*, which he began flicking through as a distraction from his woes. One morning while walking his dog on the Bondi to Malabar coastal track, Steve says he had an *epiphanous moment*. A wandering albatross thermalled up the cliff and hovered right next to him. It kept pace with Steve and his dog for several metres, expertly using its 3-metre wing span to manoeuvre in the strong currents so it could look directly into Steve's eyes. And then, in a flash, the albatross was gone, catching an upward current and disappearing behind a headland.

Steve knew the encounter was special. It's very rare to see a wandering albatross where he did – and, disappointingly, he's never seen one since. The interaction with this magnificent bird was a fateful one. It snapped Steve out of his denial and made him reflect on the damage his behaviour was causing himself and those around him.

Steve believes birds are a great metaphor for life. They represent our personalities in their simplest form. *If you think bird calls are all innocence and sweetness, think again*, he says. What birds are really saying in their dawn chorus is a riff on two basic themes: *Stay away from my territory* and *I want some sex now.* Aggression + reproduction = survival.

As if on cue, a bird starts cooing above us. We can see it perched on a branch, head and body merging into a pompom of feathers with eyes. It's a tawny frogmouth calling to its mate. It sets off two rainbow lorikeets who whiz past low and fast along the road, egging each other on with ear-piercing screeches. Otherwise, the bird activity around my tree is disappointingly docile today. The figbirds are nowhere to be seen. Even the miner birds have been called elsewhere. (I blame the cops.) Steve reminds me that this is just the nature of nature. *It* determines the schedule of things, not us. A little earlier in the morning and the scene here could have resembled an annual general meeting.

Steve's interest in birds led to a ten-part documentary series for ABC Radio called *Bird Brain,* where he delved deeper into this secret world. It helped him learn new things and focus on something other than his broken life.

While he was getting a bird's-eye view of the world, he found a species he could relate to – the superb fairy-wren. It's found in the eastern states, where it forages and builds its nests in low scrub. When it's mating, the male superb fairy-wren changes colour from brown to a blinding iridescent blue – a kamikaze-like transformation that also makes it dangerously more visible to predators. *No gain without risk.* Steve describes the male superb fairy-wren – a little too admiringly – as the world's most adulterous lothario because it needs just two seconds to have sex. Sowing your seed widely apparently stops inbreeding. It would also make for some rather complex love relationships, rivalling Steve's own.

Superb fairy-wrens aren't like most birds though. In fact, Australia is an unusual hotspot for birds that build cooperative, long-term relationships. Parrots, cockatoos – even the prickly magpie – strengthen their bonds by preening, roosting and flying together. Just as for humans, a lifelong commitment seems to prolong a species' survival.

Even in death the ties are strong. Steve once witnessed an extraordinary scene on his suburban street in Bondi. A magpie had been killed by a passing car and its body lay stiff and lifeless in the middle of the road. Several other magpies had gathered round the body, staring with heads bowed – a phenomenon ornithologists refer to as a bird *roadside funeral*. Steve says to observe wild birds mourning the death of another in this way was one of his most sorrowful encounters. Do birds experience grief the way humans do? The jury is still out on that one, say the researchers. What seem like displays of maternal or kinship mourning may simply be confusion.

While birdwatching helped Steve put his life back on track and fire up his creativity again, there were other bruising griefs to follow. His mother died a few years later – a significant loss for an only child – and the relationship that ended his marriage mellowed into a platonic friendship. There is still a melancholy about Steve as he shares these painful stories with me, and as we pack away our birdwatching outpost, I wonder how long grief keeps you imprisoned in its suffocating grip.

Will Stargirl's death cast a forever shadow over me, blocking just enough light so each new experience feels a little grey and hollow? Or can nature be an alchemist, transforming my sorrow into the beauty I see around me?

Wherever my grief takes me, I hope its final resting place is not like the magpie's, lying lifeless, alone in the middle of a deserted suburban street.

CHAPTER 11

Ice Cream and Apartheid

We're speeding down Tasmania's Midland Highway, possibly a little too fast for the road conditions, the prospect of missing our Christmas Day flight to New Zealand edging closer to an unthinkable reality.

Drive faster! urges Stargirl jumping up and down on the back seat as Dad puts his foot on the brake, expertly avoiding a dead wallaby. *Screeeeeeeeeeeech!* That was close, as more dead wallabies and wombats appear after the next turn, like a macabre obstacle course.

Sit down and put your seatbelt back on! And Indira, stop pinching your sisters. Parental tempers are fraying. If we don't make this flight, our two-week drive holiday around New Zealand's South Island will look as dead as the roadkill.

This stretch of the Midlands in Tasmania between Launceston and Hobart is nothing short of a massacre site – hundreds of native critters perish along here every week, attempting the dangerous dash to the other side. After a country drive most motorists stop at the servo to clean their dusty windscreens – Tasmanians need heavy-duty water hoses for their bumper bars.

When we first moved here from London, the animal carnage was unbearable to see. Now, we're almost as immune as the locals, barely blinking as the car speeds past a crow pecking at a bloated possum carcass upturned on the side of the road. Only Stargirl covers her eyes.

The traffic has thankfully thinned out and we've made it to the outskirts of the little colonial village of Oatlands in good time. *The Land of the Wrong White Crowd* – as Dad refers to New Zealand – may still be within our grasp *if you stop your whining and sit quietly.*

Stargirl has the grumps because our usual stop here to break up the tedious three-hour drive has been sidelined to shave off some travel time. It means she won't get to see the *hedge creatures*. Dozens of hedges, at intervals along the roadside, have been expertly clipped into animal shapes – some as high as 5 metres. They hide in the long grass, camouflaged as they would be on the savannah or in the jungles of their natural habitat. As you drive closer, each animal magically materialises from the undergrowth, behind a turn or beyond a rise.

Among the menagerie of our favourite topiary animals is a towering giraffe with legs so high you can walk between them, an alligator with snapping jaws and snarling teeth, a startled moose, a dozing koala, several birds, and – Stargirl's favourite, the only non-animal in the group – a steam engine she can actually sit in because she is so little and light. *Toot! Toot!* She doesn't seem to mind the pokey bits. A stop and thorough inspection of each one is essential for maximum awe factor.

The identity of the person behind these hedge creatures fascinates us. *How come they're here? Who made them?* we pester.

The Hedge Fairy, say our parents winking at each other, unwittingly prompting more pestering.

But where is she? Why haven't we seen her? Can we stay until she comes out? Maybe we should leave her a drink or a sandwich in case she gets hungry? Is she pretty?

So, of course, the reason we look forward so much to those drives to Hobart is to catch the elusive Hedge Fairy in action, snipping away with her shears, keeping each animal perfectly pruned. Stargirl is the keenest to spot *Fairy Scissorhands*. She would like to put a request directly to her – can the next hedge be an octopus, please?

(It isn't until decades later that I discover that these extraordinary animals – 100 in total – were created in the 1960s by a real-life hedge fairy, highway patrolman Jack Cashion. He was never commissioned to make them and continued, in his spare time, to keep them immaculately trimmed until his death in the 1990s. I wish I could have thanked him for the joy he gave us.)

We have just under two hours remaining before the plane takes off from Hobart airport for Christchurch, with still one hour of solid driving time ahead of us. *It's not looking good.* Speed cameras are some way off into the future though, so I assume we arrive at the terminal on time because the speed limit has been used as a *guide* only.

We find a long-term parking bay, suitcases are tagged and thrown on a luggage trolley, passports and plane tickets flashed, and up the metal stairs we scamper, jockeying to bags a seat near a window. We're chattering like excited zoo animals as we buckle ourselves in, testing every switch and button we can reach – from the air vents to the seat recliner – and rifling through the seat pocket for the sick bag that I blow up and pop like a balloon to scare Stargirl. She gives a satisfying startled yelp.

The air hostess shoots me a disapproving look as she hands out the special Christmas Day menu card. It's the stuff of childhood dreams. *Food on a tray.* There are slices of turkey, stuffing, roast vegies, gravy, a bread roll and a slab of jelly-custard cheesecake, all in tiny compartments, each with its own lid, fitting neatly together like an edible jigsaw. The metal salt and pepper shakers, resembling miniature Daleks, are souvenired, and kick around in the bottom of my suitcase for many years after.

As we circle Christchurch, we're disappointed to see that New Zealand isn't the exotic foreign country we were hoping for. It looks just like Tasmania. Rolling green fields disappearing into diamond blue seas. Instead of woolly blankets of sheep though, there are black-and-white cows crammed into every corner. We've never seen so many cows. There's even one at the end of the runway.

They're not the locals we're interested in seeing. We're secretly hoping to catch a glimpse of those imposing warriors with long tongues and scary tattoos we've seen on TV before the rugby matches. *No sightings yet but our eyes are peeled.*

We find our hire car, spread out the road map on the bonnet and are soon navigating our way out of the city centre, onto the open road, heading for our first stop of the night. It's only then, when we pull over at a petrol station to fill up, that the true purpose of our 'holiday' is revealed to us.

We're shown a packet of stickers. They're oval-shaped, like a football, with pictures of a rugby ball and a cricket bat and the words *Don't Play with Apartheid* printed on them. Our parents have dual identities. Dentist and homemaker by day – masked avengers committed to toppling the apartheid regime in South Africa by night.

Dad explains that the South African rugby team, the Springboks, will be touring New Zealand soon, and many people don't want a sports team that excludes black people to play against other countries. Our job during this 'holiday' is to attach these stickers wherever we can – in phone booths, on telegraph poles, on shop windows, so people will see them and join the boycott of the Springboks tour. We have to be careful though. What we are being asked to do is against the law. We can't let anyone catch us or we'll be fined for illegal bill-posting. Our parents' role is to drive the getaway car.

The thought of breaking the law terrifies us. *How can a parent ask us to do this?* Dreamcatcher, Stargirl and I are very quiet as we absorb the details of our secret mission. As the silence stretches, Dad throws in the clincher. *For every sticker you put up you can have an ice cream.*

We've seen huge billboards along the highway advertising New Zealand's prize-winning ice cream made from the pasture-rich cream from all those cows. Images of gigantic cones topped with huge melting scoops in candy colours tantalise us at every traffic light. Every street seems to have an ice-cream shop with huge icy-cold metal tubs constantly being replenished. There are exotic flavours we could never imagine . . . boysenberry, rainbow, and what the heck is hokey pokey? *Be still our beating hearts.*

Our ice cream exposure to date has been woefully limited. It's a standard weekly supermarket tub of neapolitan, with its three equal sections of industrially produced chocolate, strawberry and vanilla. We've always eaten the flavours we've been randomly assigned to avoid any fighting – Dreamcatcher always has chocolate, I get vanilla and Stargirl has strawberry. To be allowed to explore a more exotic ice-cream range makes our eyes as wide as dessert bowls. It's a dastardly bribe for a dentist father to offer. Of course, we all say yes.

Ice Cream and Apartheid

We set off to look for our first location. It's a low-risk target with no civilians in sight. A roadside phone box. Even with the promise of an ice cream, Dreamcatcher and I are petrified to be the first to venture out into this world of crime. We've seen the television news shows. This is how delinquency begins. Before we know it, we'll be prostitutes living in a heroin den.

As we hesitate, the other passenger door flies open. Stargirl races out in a flash, as brazen as can be, and slaps a sticker on the door of the phone box. Before anyone can say anything she's back in the car, heart racing with exhilaration, a big beaming smile on her face. *I'd like a scoop of hokey pokey now,* she says, showing the big girls how it's done. It is at this precise moment that I know she will always be this daring and courageous and foolhardy. Striking where others hesitate. The risk as addictive as the prize.

That summer in New Zealand, football-shaped anti-apartheid stickers mysteriously appear in shop windows, on petrol bowsers and on park benches along the tourist stretch between Christchurch and Dunedin. We watch the television news most nights after we check in to our motels and are relieved the culprits continue to elude the authorities.

We consume so much ice cream during that trip that we eventually reach a state no child has reached before: *peak ice cream.* Any subsequent ice-cream billboards we pass elicit exaggerated groans and stomach-holding.

It was Stargirl who led the way that day, only partly motivated by ice cream, exposing the ugly veneer of South Africa's apartheid regime. I will admire and fear this streak of wildness many times until her very last act of defiance breaks our hearts – and her own.

You do the hokey pokey and you turn around – is that what it's all about?

CHAPTER 12

Weeds in the Cracks

The streets of Potts Point are a hive of activity this morning.

Hundreds of pooches are taking their owners for a walk. There are furry ones, and clipped ones, some dainty, some bumbling, some furtive, others recalcitrant – and the dogs come in all shapes and sizes as well.

Finding the perfect spot for the morning ablutions seems to be the most pressing matter at hand. The best poles and trees and overgrown weeds have attracted queues as long as those for an Eastern Suburbs auction. Particularly around a tree magnolia on the footpath outside the Challis Avenue laundromat. It doesn't seem like prime toilet real estate to me, but a sizeable puddle is already forming when I stroll past, looking more intently at the world of footpaths than I would normally care to.

You see, I'm on a hunt for weeds today. Not just any weeds. But *edible* weeds. You wouldn't eat these weeds here, in the dog puddles, but the wild weeds near my fig tree have slowly opened my eyes to the wonders of the tiny unseen – those miraculous urban survivors, many of which thrive underfoot. That 2-kilometre route to the Royal Botanic Garden is now so well trod for me, every tree, every stone – even *every crack* – is etching itself into my muscle memory.

It's how I've noticed the microscopic plants pushing through the gaps in the damp stone walls around the St Vincent's schoolyard. It's how I've been captivated by the thick, lush vines that entwine themselves around the railing as I puff my way up the McElhone Stairs. It's how I marvel at two trees – seemingly strangled by the Navy carpark and a high-traffic road – still flowering and fruiting with hundreds of olive-like berries. *Even in this unforgiving landscape, nature will always find a way of asserting itself.* I've wondered how these trees and plants are able to thrive here with so little. We collectively disparage them as *weeds*, but I'm in awe of their adaptability and resilience. They are survivors.

I want to be a survivor like them. As I struggle to reassemble my broken insides, I'm willing them to give up their secrets. Which is why I've asked Sydney's most famous edible weed forager to accompany me on my urban nature walk this morning.

When I interviewed Diego Bonetto on my radio show, his exuberance for these much-maligned plants and his defence of their intrinsic value was infectious. I asked him how safe these plants were to consume. He said, *People often say to me 'Diego, why would I eat plants that dogs may have pissed on?' I say to them, 'Do you know what has been sprayed on your supermarket vegetables? Those chemicals are a lot worse than a little dog pee! Just rinse your weeds under water as you would your vegetables.'*

Diego arrives dressed like one of those dapper Italian truffle-hunters you see on television food shows. He's wearing a woven woollen cap, a long-sleeved salmon-coloured T-shirt under a navy-blue jumper and khaki vest, with grey brushed-cotton slacks and brown hiking shoes to complete the ensemble. No matter their occupation, Italians always seem ready for a fashion shoot, don't they? Diego could easily be on the cover of *Town and Country* magazine. He's lean and fit, with tanned skin and eyes ready to laugh and cry at the same time.

He knows we're on a weed hunt today, but intuitively Diego asks me why I'm writing a book specifically about nature and healing. Unprepared for the directness of his question so early on in our trek, I blurt it out in a rush of words and chest heaves, about Stargirl and her suicide, right there in the middle of the footpath, surrounded by dogs and leashes and water bowls and distracted owners.

Diego's soft brown eyes immediately begin tearing up, making me cry as well behind my sunglasses. *I am so sorry,* he says gently, crushed by this news. *My heart breaks for you.*

Thank you, I say, aware that this almost-stranger and I have fast-tracked our friendship with the sharing of this intimate grief. My reluctance not to say what has happened isn't because of shame, although I understand why shame swirls around a suicide; everyone wants someone or something to blame, so we fear people will blame us. Hell, *we* blame ourselves – why wouldn't others? We claw desperately for a simplified explanation with no loose ends and a bow on top, like a present that can be slipped under the tree, all neat and tidy and sorted. *Not to be opened until Christmas.* But suicide can't be boxed. It leaves a wreckage in its wake. Hundreds of shattered pieces from the detonation strewn like shards of jagged glass, blocking all the escape routes – unless you're prepared for your feet to be lacerated as you flee the crime scene.

Why would I want this personal horror to traumatise another soul, to up-end another with an event that has derailed my own existence? My grief counsellor, Wendy Liu, is convincing me otherwise. When I'm ready, she says, *sharing can be healing.* The professional broadcaster in me isn't wholly convinced yet. I would feel compelled to end every encounter with that warning: ... *and if anything in this conversation with me raises any issues for you, please contact Lifeline on 13 11 14.* My life has become a community service announcement.

Diego is thankfully unaware of my chaotic interior dialogue as we set off towards the Royal Botanic Garden,

Weeds in the Cracks

my burden lessened, while I guiltily suspect his shoulders seem a little heavier. We soon fall into step with each other, comrades in arms, focusing on a mission today that we *can* tackle – the hunt for edible weeds. *Our stars in the gutters.*

With the skies clear and the sun warm and embracing, everyone we pass seems to be lingering a little longer, reluctant to walk faster to the office or wrap up their morning coffee. Luckily, Diego and I have the luxury of time, to allow the day to reveal its secrets at its own pace. Play can only happen when you escape the grip of time. It's delicious knowing the city has no hold on us – for the next few hours at least – as we disappear down Challis Avenue heading towards the magic forest.

Most urban dwellers will never see the treasures we're hunting for today. Culpable, as I used to be, eyes glued to our devices, careless footsteps trampling the urban undergrowth. Diego calls it *plant blindness.* He says the foraging classes he conducts through the suburbs and along coastlines are important because once you know the name of a plant or a tree you can no longer ignore it. Give something a name and it will always demand to be seen.

Even the majestic plane trees above us have value beyond their shade. Their sap can be tapped for a syrup similar to maple syrup (although you'd need to be patient and it would only be a small quantity). Pharmaceutically, plane trees are medicine cabinets. Some people boil the

bark in vinegar for the treatment of toothache and diar-
rhoea. Their leaves may also be bruised and applied to the
eyes to treat conjunctivitis and other inflammations.

As Diego says this he suddenly pulls up abruptly, and
excitedly points out the vine I've long admired, twisting
around the railing of the McElhone Stairs. It's called
madeira, a South American émigré classed as a highly
invasive weed that is choking native vegetation all along
Australia's subtropical coast. Diego explains it's a hardy
perennial that enjoys scaling trees and then hanging
in wide curtains of heart-shaped leaves and flowers.
What many disparaging articles about it won't tell you
is that it is also edible. It's eaten extensively in Japan,
according to wild food and permaculture expert Kirsten
Bradley from Milkwood. It's known as *okawakame* or
land seaweed. Its bright-green leaves are used like a
spinach in stir-fries, and the vine's roots can be baked
like potatoes. As well as being nutritious, madeira has
highly prized medicinal qualities and is used in Chinese
medicine as an anti-inflammatory, and as an anti-ulcer
and liver protectant. *Why do we spray these when we
could harvest and cook them?* Diego asks, shaking his
head in frustration.

Within metres of this vine, at the bottom of the
McElhone Stairs, is a seemingly overgrown corner
wedged between a carpark and a road that to the
untrained eye looks like a wasteland needing a good
council clean-up. But to the eyes of a weed forager, this

is a tiny pocket of gold. As we explore the shadows and crevices, Diego darts from one spot to the next, pointing out dozens of edible plants that to me look like your everyday variety of boring grass or thistle.

No, no, says Diego exasperatedly. *This is a supermarket of free food. Look at this wood sorrel, and here pepper cress or flick weed, and then over here is a patch of dandelions, a great detoxer, mildly diuretic and aids liver function and digestion. And here's some rambling dock, which can sell for $14 a bunch!*

Two people waiting at the bus stop are watching our behaviour with concern. Yes, we're intoxicated, but not in the way they fear. Diego's excitement is infectious. I feel myself giddy too, with the variety and volume of edible plants around us. I notice that I've even started tippy-toeing behind Diego, conscious of not trampling the delicacies underfoot. *Good, good*, he says. *I wondered when the weeds would change the way you walk. It happens to most people I share this with.*

He suddenly crouches in the clearing, eye-level to a patch of small flowering plants with little white flowers. He's found some shepherd's purse – part of the mustard family. Diego says the Chinese community loves this edible and uses it to add a peppery note to salads and stir-fries. I nibble a leaf and taste the hotness straight away.

Spreading nearby in dozens of wheel spokes are patches of flatweed, popular in Greek cooking. I spent many weekends of my childhood helping my parents pull these out of the lawn and throwing them on the compost heap when we should have been throwing them into a stockpot. *One person's weed is another's delicacy.*

On the edge of this outdoor market is another edible with white-petalled flowers. It's called chickweed and it can be cooked like spinach. We must have stumbled across more than twenty edible weeds in this little quarter alone. These weeds are showing me that there's living to be had here *if you're willing to grab it by the reins and hold on for dear life.*

Diego began building his knowledge of weeds back home in Italy. He grew up on a farm, helping his parents on their smallholding. He tended the cows and pigs and looked after the vegetable garden. His family grew everything they needed – only going to the store in town for olive oil or flour. His love of foraging came from his mum, who taught him about the abundance of free food in the surrounding fields and forests. He scampered through the brambles collecting blackberries, fennel and nettles. And in autumn there were mushrooms hiding under the pine needles. From roots and berries to plants and fungi, the wild foods of the Italian countryside were never seen as weeds; they were culinary delights, free and tasty.

As we reach my tree, Diego points out more edibles poking up through the cracks of the bush rock. There are tiny fronds of fat hen, which can be baked into bread. Further along, in a large patch on the sloping grass, are yellow dandelions, chickweed and more flatweed. Now that Diego has opened my eyes, it's as if I can only see edibles. My plant blindness has been cured in a matter of hours.

With our forage deemed a standout success, we make our way back through the Gardens to Macleay Street to grab some breakfast. Bouncing gayly in my hand are two posies of edibles I can take back home to study further.

If your love of life is faltering, a weed will certainly set you straight. I've seen life sprouting in places I thought it would be impossible to survive. Indigenous Australian writer and farmer Uncle Bruce Pascoe says that when you *ingest a plant you metabolise its story*. The story of weeds is one of survival, determination and resilience. Their domain in the city may be within the cracks, but cracks are also how the light gets in.

CHAPTER 13

Peas in a Pod

0500 hours.

Getting ready for school is a military operation requiring obedience, discipline and stamina. *I didn't know the word 'dawdle' existed until years later.* I'm not saying we always met these key performance indicators. All I can say in our defence is that we had a lot to pack in for little kids. We were overscheduled before the term was even invented.

Mum too easily slips into the role of Siegfried from *Get Smart*: *You vill be on zime!* Whitey, our tenant's cat (guess what colour she is?), plays the role of Kaos agent Chief Distraction, curling her tail between our legs, purring enticingly and then rolling on her back, demanding a tummy rub while we're trying to brush our teeth. Stargirl is particularly susceptible to Whitey's sophisticated tactics.

The Space Between the Stars

Each weekday morning begins with an hour of swimming training with the school squad. We're almost always the last in the pool, even though we live across the road. The coach makes a point of embarrassing us each time. *Ah, the Naidoo girls! Honoured you could grace us with your presence. You live just 30 metres away but are always late. An extra lap for you.*

We slip off our insulating tracksuits and ugg boots (back when they were a daggy thing to wear outdoors), pull on our caps and goggles and dive into the watery bootcamp. The biting Tassie air combined with the sub-zero water temperature sends our bodies into thermal shock. It will be hours before we can feel our toes again.

We have a future Commonwealth Games medallist on the team so it's a cracking pace. *Stroke, stroke, breathe. Stroke, stroke, breathe. Stroke, stroke, breathe.* We suck in the icy air through our teeth and feel the oxygen expand our lungs. It's like a giddy shot of pseudoephedrine.

Soon the conga line of swimmers falls into a steady rhythm. Our heartbeat becomes a drum pushing us through the pain barrier. Fingertips to the toes of the swimmer in front, the robotic splashes punctuated by yells from the coach. *Push! Push harder! Keep those arms high. I want those muscles to burn.*

Up and down we go, slicing through the chill. Lap after lap, focusing on the lines of black tiles on the bottom of the pool and the churn from the kicks of the swimmer ahead of us. Slacken your pace ever so slightly and a tap on your feet from the swimmer behind will jolt you back into formation.

Your order in this amphibious chorus line is determined by your best lap time. As the youngest and slowest members of the team, the three of us are the 'tail end of the dog', so to speak. All the other swimmers are fair-skinned, so . . . *ha ha!* . . . it's a white dog with a brown tail.

Stargirl is on the cusp of being too small and too young to do this, but the grown-ups think it will be good for her. And besides – she always wants to keep up with the big girls. *No pain, no gain.*

The punishment is over after an hour. We pull our weary bodies up the metal ladder with our anaesthetised hands and feet. Wet and shivering we scramble down the street, under the spreading oaks, back home and straight into the shower.

Waiting for us in our rooms are our school uniforms, laid out on our beds, pressed to perfection – right down to our blue satin hair ribbons. *Siegfried's German efficiency.* Our winter uniforms are designed to shield us from the biting Tasmanian cold – brown woollen ribbed stockings, cloud-blue shirts, brown jumpers, tartan woollen kilted skirts, brown blazer, scarf, gloves and brown brogues. Layer upon layer upon layer – of brown.

After we're kitted up, we slide around the chunky pine kitchen table, the oil radiator going full bore, and wolf down bowls of steaming porridge sprinkled with brown sugar and a dollop of butter, before grabbing our lunch boxes, school bags, hats and coats, and piling out the door – the school bell chiming within earshot.

It feels like we've lived a day already, but it's only 0830 hours. We still have to survive piano lessons at recess, tennis play-offs at lunch and hockey after school. But we push each other through, Dreamcatcher and Stargirl and I. The Three Amigos. The Three Musketeers. The Three Sisters.

We're our own gang.

Many numerologists consider the number three the perfect number. The number of harmony, wisdom and understanding. It's also the number of time – past, present and future; birth, life and death. *The power of three.* Three is the smallest number needed to create a pattern – the perfect combination of brevity and rhythm. There's even a Latin phrase for it: *Omne trium perfectum.* It means everything that comes in threes is perfect, or every set of three is complete.

The three of us are *body, soul and spirit.*

We've never had to consider where one of us begins and the other ends. There's a well-known Australian comedy duo called the Umbilical Brothers – we are the umbilical *sisters.* We share the same blood. We breathe the same air. We wake up together, and every night, breath against cheek, our heads hit the pillow. We are each other's shadows.

Peas in a Pod

Our frequent family relocations fracture our ties to our friends and kin, but only serve to draw our bonds even tighter. Only two other souls in this whole universe share similar memories to me. Only two others remember the same taste of things – biting into that wedge of watermelon, crisp and cool straight from the esky, sticky juices running down our chins, the way the sand sparkled as we ran to the water's edge, dark and salty waves abrasive against our zinc-creamed skin.

We are three. *Slip. Slop. Slap.*

Just a year between us. As chronologically close as three siblings can be without being triplets. It gives us an invincibility like *Ajax! With triple-action cleaning power!*

So now, for our threesome to be severed after almost half a century of being psychically conjoined at the hip, feels apocalyptic. The end of everything. An unimaginable horror that none of us could have foreseen as we swam our laps in synchronicity. How could we? How could anyone?

How did a plum tree in a Melbourne suburban backyard almost fifty years later become a makeshift gallows for the brightest star in our trio? This plum tree, a symbol of life and strength and protection, was coopted into the most horrific of roles. I've been all too conscious of the striking symbolism of two sisters and their two very different relationships with their trees.

My fig tree has been giving me back my life; Stargirl used a plum tree to take away hers.

As Stargirl climbed into its branches, the night air dank and brooding, and slipped the chain around her neck, the only witness to her final precious moments was this tree. A silent sentinel that could not move, that could not scream.

The arborist comes the week after Stargirl's death to remove the tree. It's a punishment for being in the wrong place at the wrong time. Its black trunk and purple leaves are all that remain of the dark grisly deed that transpired under its branches. The arborist has seen this tragedy played out many times. He has had to remove many trees like this, trees used in this way by the agonised and tormented. Trees removed in the hope of erasing the awfulness of the memory. He knows it never works.

With the soil freshly levelled, and the mulch replaced, he departs with the strangest of comments: *It's not the tree's fault.* His breach of protocol stuns us with its candour. But he must tell his truth. Of course it's not the tree's fault. All it could do was be present.

They say everything comes in threes. What they don't tell you is that everything departs in threes as well. Dreamcatcher and I, we cannot be without the third.

The beginning, the middle and the end.

CHAPTER 14

The Shape of Things

I'm stretched out on the prickly grass near my tree, lying on my back, watching tutus of pale vanilla clouds pirouette through the sky. They glide and flounce as if worn by a troupe of unseen ballerinas performing on an aerial stage. How lovely they are!

I haven't done this since I was a kid. Just watching the clouds go by.

My sky-gazing companion on this squeaky-bright morning, Branka Spehar, points out another spot on the horizon where a bank of cloud is separating into what, to me, looks like a herd of gazelle drinking at a watering hole. Branka smiles at my description. She says she can see a turtle. Same cloud formation, two different interpretations.

I came across Branka's research on the University of New South Wales's website while I was looking for a better understanding of why we all – regardless of background – seem largely to find the same aspects of nature arresting, be it a cloud or a sunset. As a visual psychologist at the university, Professor Spehar's specialty is this *shape perception.*

Branka is one of the nature guides I've enlisted to unlock the magic of my urban world. She's helping me understand why, seemingly inexplicably, watching feathery cirrus clouds morph gently into an old woman and then into a hamster – the woman's nose becoming the hamster's hind leg – feels like the most calming activity I've engaged in for years.

While I'm trying to heal in the latest of Sydney's stay-at-home lockdowns I may not be able to hike a mountain or walk along a crashing surf beach, but I'm realising the wilderness in the skies is always within my reach. It's all too easy to dismiss clouds as a mundane presence in our urban landscape. But by doing so we become blind to their power.

As a young girl growing up in Croatia, Branka found the surrounding woodlands of pine and cypress magical, and would set off for long walks through the country-side, losing herself in the contours of the landscape. She may be in her fifties now, with a bob of dark-grey hair framing her round face, but I can still see that young girl's wide-eyed wonder as we explore the skies together, watching more clouds build up on the horizon. Ash from nearby pre-bushfire burn-offs is mixing with the warm air, forming cumulus clouds as dense as scoops of licorice ice cream. They're so close we could almost lick them.

Branka's interest in nature eventually turned into an academic pursuit. She began focusing her studies on why humans are so visually affected by their natural world. After completing her PhD in psychology, she continued her exploration of visual perception and how our senses process the beauty we see around us.

Branka's research challenges widely accepted scientific wisdom. She has found that what we find beautiful is not dictated primarily by our individual and cultural experiences – as is the prevailing view. While individuals do disagree about what they find beautiful, this is often when they are assessing a piece of art attempting to *replicate* nature. The beauty of nature itself, on the other hand, doesn't divide us so. There is general agreement, across most cultures, about the aesthetic pleasure we derive from landscapes, clouds, shimmering skies, rivers, flowers, trees, crystals or even faces. Branka's view is that we are hardwired in our DNA to find our natural surroundings beautiful. After all, it is nature that has helped us evolve and survive, so recognising this beauty is an important short cut to helping us identify the places where we can be safe and heal.

And how these parts of the natural world are physically structured holds particular allure for us. Have you ever noticed how a tree trunk splits into branches and these branches, in turn, split into smaller branches and so on and so on, in a seemingly infinitely reductive pattern? Large becomes smaller; small becomes tiny. It's a pattern of growth referred to as 'fractals', and it's a design repeated throughout nature. So while a tree, on the surface, may look very different from a river or a cloud, when you study their pattern of growth, these fractals keep recurring. Networks of large keep subdividing into networks of small. Without being consciously aware of it, we find these fractal patterns so soothing to the eye that the need to seek out natural scenes containing them becomes a subconscious compulsion.

I test Branka's theory and study my tree from our grassy vantage point, letting my eye follow its branches as they spread and split, spread and split. The simple act of running my eyes across the curves and forks of those bark tributaries is immediately relaxing. *It's a revelation.*

Branka explains that what we humans love about nature are the visual imperfections, the knobbly indentations and bumps. Machine-made structures are too linear and hard, and our eyes can't relax as they move over them. It leaves us feeling stressed. Whereas a tree and its branches allow our sight to linger and laze, prompting the rest of our body to relax while we absorb the curves and contours.

We also find it aesthetically pleasing that nothing in nature is ever still. There's always some movement in a natural setting, not too sudden but gentle – a sway, a ripple, a moving shadow, a shimmer, a buzz ... all subtle, all calming. Buildings don't move (or shouldn't), poles don't sway, concrete doesn't ripple. Their hardness and immovability disturbs us at our very core. That's why, in contrast, we can look at clouds, sunsets, bodies of water or a forest seemingly for hours. Their subtle changes hypnotise us into states of calm and bliss. Their movement is enough to engage our attention but not so changeable as to over-activate our stress receptors. It can lead to a euphoric state that writer Robert Macfarlane describes in his book *Landmarks* as *ecstatic idleness*, where immersion in nature becomes intoxicating bliss.

Branka and I watch a fresh furrow of low cloud cast a shadow over the bay. The water grows dark and moody, signalling the weather may be changing. As we gather our bags to walk back down the hill, Branka explains more about how the shape of things can deeply affect our peace of mind. Lines, she says, for example, are spiky and sharp and remind us of danger. Spiky things in nature can often hurt us or be unpleasant to touch. From a young age we instinctively know to stay away from them. We inherit this knowledge as information embedded deep in our genes, so we feel we've had a direct unpleasant experience with them before we actually have. How much of this happens subconsciously is fascinating. We need these patterns of nature hardwired into us so we can quickly identify safety or food sources. Our very survival has always depended on it.

The Space Between the Stars

As Branka and I make our way back to where we met, near the Art Gallery, she explains that beauty in nature exists to make us feel better. The natural world has been designed to give us all the pleasure we require, she explains. So when it fails to fill us with wonder, as it did with Stargirl, the darkness will come very quickly.

Aesthetics is the study of beauty in nature. The word *aesthetics* comes from the Greek for 'to perceive'. And interestingly, the opposite of aesthetic is *anaesthetic*, which means to 'lose perception and to blunt sensation'.

It was precisely what Stargirl did.

CHAPTER 15

Smiley Hairclip and Birthday Party

We can't scramble into the car fast enough, jostling for who gets the front seat. The person with the longest legs needs the most leg room. Another rule I've created. *So, of course, being the tallest, I am the beneficiary.*

We're off to McKinlay's department store in the city to be fitted for our new school uniforms. For a small town like Launceston, McKinlay's is the epitome of high-end glamour. It advertises its wares in large, moulded lettering above its entrance – *Drapers. Furnishers. Tailors.* We only step through the doors of its ornate custard-yellow façade on the rarest of occasions – when Mum needs a new cocktail dress for a fundraiser or to drop off Dad's tuxedo for dry-cleaning.

The tiled floors shimmer like black marble, so smooth and slippery we can skate in our shoes. The walls and ceiling are mirrored like a palace. The light fittings hang like flickering candles on a birthday cake. The shop assistants all wear elegant black dresses, with their hair pulled back in stylish *chignons du cous*. The older ones have tape measures around their collars and their black nylon stockings make a scratching sound when they walk. It's like being in an episode of *Are You Being Served?*.

We make our way to the top floor, where uniforms for all the city's schools are displayed on circular racks. There's Queechy High, Grammar, St Pat's and, in the far corner, our school, Broadland House.

The assistant starts measuring us up and selects some uniforms for us to try in the changerooms. We emerge transformed from scraggly summer urchins into learned scholars with straight backs and serious demeanours as we parade in front of the mirrors. We've all grown inches over the holidays, particularly Stargirl. Because she is going through a growth spurt, a uniform two sizes too big is selected for her. She looks like she's wearing one of Mum's dressing gowns. *She'll fill it out*, Mum says.

As we make our way back to the front entrance, we bump into some schoolfriends who are also with their mother preparing for back-to-school. The mums begin chattering busily while Dreamcatcher and I swap holiday stories with our classmates.

Stargirl is left to her own devices and wanders through the jewellery section admiring the sparkles and baubles. She returns, pulling at Mum's dress with big imploring eyes, holding in her hand a hairclip on its cardboard backing.

Smiley Hairclip and Birthday Party

Can I have this? she pleads, waving the metal clip in the shape of the word *smile* in coloured letters.

No, says Mum firmly. *Put it back.*

But I want it, she squeals louder.

No, says Mum, now very annoyed that her adult conversation is being interrupted. *And don't ask me again.*

Stargirl pouts and stomps her foot and walks back to the jewellery counter seemingly defeated.

When we arrive back home, Mum jumps out of the car to pull up the garage roll-a-door and Dreamcatcher races in with her. Stargirl has been very quiet during the return trip. I assume she's been sulking, but she suddenly pipes up when the coast is clear, and whispers, *If I tell you a secret do you promise not to tell Mum?*

I turn around from the front seat. *Of course,* I say, promising something I might not be able to deliver.

Stargirl puts her hand in her pocket and, with great reverence, pulls out the smiley hairclip still attached to its cardboard backing.

My eyes grow wide with horror. *Stargirl has stolen the clip! We're harbouring a felon!*

At that precise moment Mum slides back into the car and I immediately blurt out what Stargirl has done.

There is a volcanic eruption behind Mum's eyes. She orders me out of the car with the shopping and says she is driving back to the store so Stargirl can apologise and return the stolen hairclip. As the white Golf

Volkswagen speeds off back into town, I can see the look of betrayal on Stargirl's face through the back-seat window.

I'm not sure what transpires during that McKinlay's visit, but when Stargirl joins us later in the rumpus room she is wearing the smiley clip in her hair with a satisfied grin on her face. Maybe Mum got a case of the guilts. She never explains.

I am feeling guilty as well. Why had I dobbed Stargirl in, when my transgressions had set the bar at a level, several years earlier, that no five-year-old has possibly ever surpassed? Stargirl's naughtiness had nothing on mine . . .

It's early winter in London and our temp teacher is doing a roll call. It's a small class – just fifteen students, mostly from eastern European and South-East Asian back-grounds. My sixth birthday is approaching and, having discovered early what will be my lifelong love of a cele-bration, I have asked Mum if I can have a party. Mum has said an emphatic no. Money is tight with three children under six and Dad only working part-time so he can resit exams to have his dental qualifications recognised in England. Mum has promised we'll celebrate my birthday *next year*.

But I'm determined to have a party, and while the temp teacher is handing out stamps and ink pads for our next lesson, I hatch a plan. I hand-write fifteen notes, addressed to each one of my classmates, explaining that I am having a birthday party at my house this Friday. They are all to catch the school bus with me after school, and then their parents can pick them up afterwards.

I hand the notes, with my address, to the students and explain to the temp teacher that my usual class teacher, Mrs Brown, knows all about the party. The temp teacher is not the least bit suspicious.

Come Friday I am beside myself with excitement. All day we chat about the games we'll play and the birthday cake we'll eat and how much fun it's going to be. After school the temp teacher helps us all onto the bus and wishes me the best for my party. I'm beaming with anticipation. The bus drops us off on my street and I proudly lead the way up our path to the front door – fifteen hungry and excited kids dragging school bags behind me.

Being only just six and not understanding words like *ramifications* or *consequences*, I've not thought ahead about what Mum's reaction will be when she sees this merry gathering. I rap the doorknocker. Mum opens the door. She has Stargirl on her hip, feeding her a bottle. Dreamcatcher is clinging to her leg.

I say I've brought all my schoolfriends for my party. She slowly absorbs what I have done, momentarily frozen with incredulity. She recovers quickly, sizing up the situation, and starts working out how to manage this crisis.

She gathers us all inside and quickly calls a neighbour to watch us so she can dash to the corner shop to buy some biscuits and cordial.

I am blissfully unaware of my selfishness and what a dull party I have forced upon my classmates. Several kids complain that there are no games or birthday cake. Mum hastily wraps up some lollies and arranges a pass-the-parcel and a game of musical chairs on the back lawn. All the while Stargirl grumbles in her cot and Dreamcatcher shyly tries to join the action.

The two hours until the parents arrive to pick up their children must seem interminable for Mum. *Fifteen strangers' kids and three of her own.* Somehow, she keeps us all fed and entertained until the first doorbell chimes.

When we are seeing off the last child at the door, their parent asks them whether they have had a good time. This little girl speaks with the honesty of all young children. She says that it has been *the worst birthday party she has ever been to.* Her reaction doesn't worry me. My birthday couldn't have been better. But what is the look in Mum's eyes? *Embarrassment? Sadness?*

For some reason I never get the hiding I deserve for that birthday caper. Perhaps Mum is just too tired, or too guilty that she couldn't give her child a party. I'm not sure. As the terrible naughtiness of what I have done slowly filters in, I wait for days, and then weeks, but no wooden spoon ever emerges from the kitchen drawer.

Gosh, we could be such rotten kids.

Smiley Hairclip and Birthday Party

Mum taught us to be daring and fearless and single-minded in our determination. How we applied those ideals though was, of course, always going to be out of her hands.

CHAPTER 16

Garden in the Sky

It's started again.

My mind has been tossing and turning, unable to settle. No matter what I do, I can't shut it down. It seems to be fuelled by its own power pack of dark matter, constantly twisting and coiling, chasing and fleeing. One moment it's trapped like a hunted doe-eyed deer, frantically lost in a labyrinth of its own making; the next it's careering down the Luna Park roller-coaster, looking like Heath Ledger's demented Joker from *Batman*, hair wild, eyes bloodshot, screaming with the rest of the waking dead. Why won't it just . . . *s. . .t. . .o. . .p*?

The isolation of loss is the worst kind of haunting. *How do you escape from yourself?*

I've been grimly pondering my starring role in this psychological hostage drama as I sit on my balcony, hands warmed by a mug of English breakfast tea. The air is frosty this morning – there must be snow on the Blue Mountains to Sydney's west. It's made the sky the colour of steel. The wind has also picked up. It drones across the rooftops as an arrowhead of ibis shoots through, quivering in streamlined perfection. On the harbour a ferry appears from behind a curtain of fog, unfailingly cheery in its green and yellow livery. Still, the sun will have its work cut out for it if it's to convince the rest of city to venture out into this day.

I tilt my face skywards to catch a few rays of that midwinter sun. It's a delicious sensory contrast – the iciness in the breeze combined with the gentle heat on my cheeks. For a few stolen seconds the wind dips and the warmth infuses deep into my aching muscles. I feel fortified, nourished. The edges of darkness slowly begin to thaw.

The plants on my balcony are also soaking up the shards of sunshine. Their downcast leaves shimmer with renewed iridescence. I can see the delicate network of veins in their leaves backlit in the light.

How I've neglected them during these past few months!

Several punnets of wilting seedlings lie forlornly in the corner – still unplanted. Bags of unopened compost and potting mix sag against the wall, and planter boxes of summer herbs and tomatoes – long gone to seed – brown and wither on their vines and branches.

My grief has somehow constructed an invisible barrier between my writing desk and my edible plants.

And in the process, I've been blinded to one of the most powerful places for my healing to begin – my little balcony garden.

It feels so good to have my hands in the soil again. It's damp and cool and spongy – like crumbs of chocolate cake.

I've decided to finally empty out all the old pots and tubs, and plant out the tray of winter edibles. There's frilly-leaved purple kale, long tongues of English spinach, peppery rocket, rainbow-stalked silverbeet, a few tightly furled gem lettuces, some sweet basil, and a tube of heart-sease violas to keep the pollinators happy.

First, all the bamboo stakes need to be removed, bundled up and stored away for the next tomato season. Then the remnants of my summer crops need to be evicted. I start ripping out the dead vines at their roots, enjoying the vigour required to dislodge them. I'm already building up a sweat. A few juicy caterpillars are shaken from their hidey-holes. They curl and squirm as I pick them up and drop them into a nearby spider's web. That's dinner sorted! *Gardens are not places for the timid.*

Pottering away in this tiny nook in the sky over the past few years, I've learned some pertinent lessons about life and death and how survival is never guaranteed. I can tenderly plant all these seedlings and nurture them attentively, watering and weeding, and still some will not make it.

And yet here I am, trowel in hand, mixing fresh potting mix and compost into my tubs with the optimism of a first-time gardener. And at its crux that's the addiction of anyone with the garden bug: the chance to play God in a small way, to give life to something that would not have had that opportunity without your intervention.

I've reached some stubborn roots in my largest planter box. They belong to a last-season silver-green broccoli head that has flowered and seeded and is now determinedly anchored in place. My persistent tugs and grunts just won't budge it. Time to use a tool in the gardener's arsenal rarely deployed in a potted balcony garden – a long-handled spade.

In it goes, slicing through the fibrous roots, until I can feel some give from the stalk. A little more pulling and tugging and finally it surrenders, but not without taking a large clump of soil with it. The soil is much more alive and vital down here where the roots have formed an underground network of hundreds of hair-like capillaries. I stop my strenuous clearing for a bit and inhale deeply. I find the aroma of damp soil so intoxicating. It's possibly why I love gardening so much.

And its seductive powers appear to be universal.

There are physiological reasons why we find this musty smell or *geosmin* particularly pleasurable. Geosmin is created by bacteria that live deep in the soil. When the perfume of these compounds hits the prehistoric parts of our olfactory centre, it signals that food and water are nearby. It's why when we smell damp soil our mood lifts immediately. *It's the aroma of life.* There's also considerable research showing that these compounds act in a similar way to antidepressant pills.

It's possibly why I've never met an unhappy gardener.

My serotonin levels must be rising too. I have to temper my excitement as I slide each seedling out of its plastic tub and furrow a small planting hole in the soil with a cupped hand. I'll regret it if I rush this stage. I could damage the tender roots and shoots. *I'm clumsy at the best of times.* In goes each seedling, carefully spaced to give room for those roots to grow deep and strong. I level out the soil around each stem and press down firmly, as if I'm tucking little ones into bed.

I stand back to admire my labour. All up, I've filled one large planter and two large tubs. A tiny vegie patch by anyone's measure, but to me it's an abundant acreage of joy. Right here at my fingertips, these fragile beauties will grow and bush up, hopefully only needing the occasional caress from me. They must weather the pests and diseases largely by themselves. I can assist but I can't control. I'm trusting that my garden assistants – air, sunlight and water – will do the rest. And if they do survive, I will have deep gratitude for the bounty they'll provide. I can harvest free, delicious greens whenever I need to elevate a salad or whip up a pesto. *My supermarket in the sky.*

I grab the hose to fill up the watering can. I'm covered in dirt right up to my elbows but it feels cleansing and cathartic. I've been so deeply engrossed in my plants and imagining the life they'll have, that I haven't noticed the sun dipping behind the city towers. The dark will come quickly now.

I give the seedlings a deep soaking, watching tiny droplets of water skip off their tender shoots and slide down towards their roots. There, beneath the surface, unseen, a remarkable alchemy will take place. A transformation that began long before animals roamed this place. As the plant's leaves capture and convert the sunlight into carbohydrates, the roots will draw up water and minerals in just the right amounts to nourish these sprouts. Plants are a cosmic lesson in how you can find all you need precisely where you are. It is why plants are the powerhouse of the planet.

My final job before I pack away my afternoon of potting is to label my new crop. As I begin plunging each white plastic marker into the soil I suddenly recoil. Why have I never seen the symbolism before? *These plant labels resemble headstones protruding from freshly dug graves.*

There is a meaning here for me. I try to sit with the discomfort.

Gardening is not only an act of hope; it is also an act of acceptance. Endings are part of renewal. You can't have one without the other. Gardens are where we sign a pact with nature; nature will do its bit, and we'll do ours. Yes, something may die but something will grow as well.

We can't ask for more than that.

CHAPTER 17

Dad's Toupee

We thunder down the stairs, in a tizz of excitement, to see if the taxi has arrived. No sighting yet.

The hallway is lined with our bags – the entire possessions of a family of five squeezed into six scuffed brown and blue leather suitcases and three boxes. To a six-year-old it looks like a lot of stuff. I badger my mother for the umpteenth time. *Will Mary be all right?* My overriding concern is for Mary, my favourite doll, who is packed away in there somewhere with her milk bottle and pink hairbrush. My frazzled mother says she'll put *me* in there *with Mary* if I don't behave and look after my sisters.

For our long flight to our new home in Australia, Dreamcatcher, Stargirl and I have been dressed immaculately – as always. We're in matching outfits in three different sizes. Red-and-black-checked jumpsuits with frilled-ribboned white socks and black patent-leather shoes. Our hair is pulled back neatly into pigtails. With her bulky nappy filling out the bottom of her jumpsuit, Stargirl waddles around looking like a mini version of the robot from *Lost in Space*.

I have been instructed to keep a firm grip on Stargirl's hand at all times. *We'll be busy with passports and immigration,* explain my parents. Clutching on to that chubby little sticky hand is deeply etched into my memory of that day that went on forever, as we shuffled through the long queues at Heathrow airport, to be finally swallowed up into the mouth of a huge jumbo jet, shuddering off the runway, higher and higher into the clouds until the people and cars on the ground became microscopic specks, like trails of busy ants. There's a memory flash of a drowsy stopover in Singapore, breathing in air like steam from a hot bath, before being herded back onto the plane to our final destination – Hobart, Tasmania. *The arse end of the world?* Not to me.

The medicinal aroma of eucalyptus hits my nostrils as we step out onto the tarmac. *Instinctively, I know this is where I'm meant to be.* I squint through the piercing morning light at the soft mauve hills and the sheep grazing along the fence line. I'm an inner-city London kid. This is the closest I've ever been to a sheep. I'm surprised at how similar they look to the ones I've made in school using cottonwool, black pipe-cleaners and a cardboard toilet roll. We're staying overnight in a hotel near the Derwent River, before we make the drive to our new home in the little town of St Marys on the east coast.

Dad's Toupee

The new day will bring an even bigger change: we wake to discover our father without any hair! His thick black Elvis-like quiff has disappeared overnight to be replaced by a smooth shiny dome. *I've shaved it all off,* Dad explains. *New country. Felt like a change. Besides – what you don't have on the outside you have on the inside!* This new-look father is a lot to get used to. Stargirl is still not sure who he is and hides behind Mum's legs, eyeing the imposter suspiciously. Soon we are bundled into a hire car, heading over the gentle span of the Tasman Bridge, up the Midland Highway, then the Esk Highway to St Marys for the next leg of our over-adventurous life.

Years later, in another home nearby in Launceston, we find ourselves banished to the rumpus room downstairs while our parents entertain some important guests visiting from overseas. Heavy rain is falling, creating muddy rivulets on the dusty windows. We can't ride our bikes, the trampoline is off limits – leaving just the piano for entertainment. We soon tire of *chopsticks threeways* and begin exploring a hoard of old boxes we discover in the garage storeroom.

There's a goldmine in here! There are whoops of laughter as we find items of clothing we recognise from our parents' old photo albums. *Dress-ups has never been so much fun!* Dreamcatcher finds an old maxi dress covered in a large brown-and-yellow daisy print and matches it with some blue denim wedges and a pink sun hat. I rummage around the bottom of another box and discover a long blue satin skirt, black pumps and a white fur shrug.

Stargirl has crawled into another larger box and disappears almost completely, feverishly burrowing her way through coats and jumpers, ski boots and swimsuits until she unearths the dress-up prize of the afternoon. At first, we're perplexed by this triangular brown wedge of plastic covered in black fur. Is it the old seat of a bicycle? Perhaps it's a cap. Then its provenance slowly dawns upon me.

It's Dad's hair!

We're a little disturbed by what this means as we throw it between each other like a frisbee, *eeking!* and *yukking!* as we run our fingers over the coarse black hair and hard plastic underside that once sat atop Dad's head.

Stargirl balances the toupee on top of her own hair and begins doing a pretend catwalk with exaggerated hip swings and pouting lip poses. And then the naughtiest of smiles slowly flickers across her face. Before Dreamcatcher and I can block her escape, she has darted out the garage door, back into the house, bounding up the stairs into the living room where our parents are. We follow in hot pursuit secretly looking forward to how much trouble Stargirl is going to get into for this audacious stunt. This will be a lot worse than the wooden-spoon hiding I got for setting the bedspread on fire.

As Stargirl blows into the room, our embarrassed parents recognise the accoutrement immediately – as do their guests – and fumble for an explanation. *I started losing my hair in my twenties*, Dad explains. *The toupee was a bad idea that I tried and ditched when we moved to Tasmania.* He attempts a chuckle but his vanity has been exposed and he has nowhere to hide. It's the first time we have seen our father vulnerable and a little broken. The next time will be during my eulogy for Stargirl, when our eyes meet and I wonder if this is one of the many memories of Stargirl that is flashing through his mind as well.

His baby girl departing this world before he does.

A wife who loses a husband is called a widow. A husband who loses a wife is called a widower. A child who loses their parents is called an orphan.

Why is there no word for a parent who loses a child?

Is it because it goes against what nature intended? Or is it that the loss is so profound, the heartbreak so seismic, we believe that if there is no word for a terrible thing, perhaps we can ensure it will not to happen to us?

I came across a Sanskrit word, not in mainstream English usage, that goes some way to describing the incapacitating anguish a parent must feel. The word is *vilomah* and it means *against the natural order* – the grey-haired should never bury those with dark hair.

Hair is often mythologised as a symbol of strength and invincibility, but Stargirl's lustrous locks could not protect her in the end. And with Stargirl gone, my father's still shiny dome will now need to double as a shield.

CHAPTER 18

The Secret Life of Puddles

I love to watch the way rain makes pedestrians in the city scatter. Suddenly shoulders tense, collars are up, and brollies are deployed, flapping open like the black leathery wings of a cauldron of bats, darting under awnings, zigzagging dangerously across traffic, all to avoid getting a little wet.

When the rains come in the bush, the images couldn't be more different – particularly after a long period of drought. There's jubilant yahooing, shy farmers water-sliding in their underwear through the muddy torrents, tinnies cracked open, livelihoods saved from ruin. *Tears from heaven.*

I can relate to those pedestrians. I don't like getting wet either when I'm clothed, but remember when we were little? You couldn't keep us away from water, could you?

Despite our parents' warnings, water had a magnetic pull in all its forms: from oceans to rivers, swimming pools to sprinklers, taps, hoses, baths, to the most forbidden reservoir of them all – puddles.

I just love saying that word. *Puddle.*

Puddles may have looked innocent, but to our parents they were a silent menace. They were filthy and muddy and could swallow up little children who would never be clean again. *Ever.*

And then we *became* those parents.

I hadn't thought about puddles for ages until my regular hikes to my fig tree began to give the ground beneath my feet new significance. Why had I forgotten how captivating the world down there could be? Feathers, weeds and now puddles were where infinite joy could be found.

After a downpour I love to see where fresh puddles have sprung up or where old puddles have returned. That little uneven depression on the bitumen path near Harry's Café de Wheels, where the pigeons preen and splash, has become a favourite, or the long flat puddle on the sandstone steps leading to the Gardens near the Wool-loomooloo marina that reflects the sky like Alice's looking glass. Mirrored portals to another dimension – that's how I like to think of puddles.

The real magic, though, happens when raindrops fall on a puddle, creating a mesmerising surface dance of fading circles. The rain and the puddle morph into globules of liquid mercury, lifting and collapsing like ballerinas in a production of *Swan Lake*.

There's actually a lot of science to a puddle. These little pools of wetness are far from random. Where they form, how long they stay and why they vanish are all choreographed by nature. Puddles consist of small, naturally formed ridges (*berms*) and depressions (*swales*). The berms form from a build-up of silt and leaf litter, and act like mini dam walls that trap water behind them in the swales. Puddles love depressions and dips – usually on the edges of paths where the surface is uneven. A pothole in a road is prime puddle real estate, and so are the craggy surfaces of a broken footpath.

Our risk-averse obsession with concreting and flattening over everything has destroyed much of a puddle's natural habitat. But when a puddle does miraculously materialise, the local wildlife swoops like it's knock-off time at the front bar. Watch a puddle for a bit and you'll be surprised by what a busy watering hole it becomes.

There's a puddle that appears, after the rain, on the edge of a slab of lichen-covered bush rock near my tree. Word gets out within minutes. *Hey, fellas! The puddle's back!* Soon there are magpies, noisy miners and long-necked herons enjoying a drink or washing off their dusty feathers. And sometimes if they're lucky there may be a tasty worm or two wriggling up from their burrows for a little air. This shared bathing time is something to behold. It's as if a ceasefire has been declared. The usual pecking and squawking are suspended so everyone can enjoy a little puddle time. Of course, if the puddles are deep ones there are also tadpoles and mosquito larvae swimming around, hoping the puddle stays around long enough for them to reach adulthood.

I've marvelled at the rich biodiversity a tiny puddle can support. Even plants depend on them. That's not just dust on the surface. They are microscopic seed pods lubricating themselves in those muddy ripples, using the puddle's serendipitous arrival as an opportunity to germinate. So much life in such a tiny receptacle.

I've come across a fascinating term involving puddles, following one of my monthly grief-counselling sessions with Wendy. The state of leaping in and out of grief is known as *puddle-jumping*. It's been given this name because children are more likely to be affected by this form of bereavement. One moment they're flat and uncommunicative, the next they're skipping and laughing with their friends.

I've experienced similar grief swings since Stargirl died. Present in a conversation one moment, then disappearing the next.

Just like a puddle.

Could puddles be more than just a metaphor for grief, though, and be an actual cure? The power of puddles to heal us may not be as strange as it sounds. Rather than view puddles as an inconvenience or an annoyance as most adults do, children see them as magical places of endless joy. Maybe if we could recapture that state, the healing would follow.

Our granddaughter Abbie may have some insights. When I was researching the various experts I could chat to about puddles (and yes, puddles are an actual area of academic study), I realised no one could know more about puddles than an eight-year-old girl. When I asked Abbie if she would like to accompany me on a walk to my tree to explore some puddles, she was delighted by the invitation and not in the least surprised that a grown-up would want to do this with her. Her only request for our morning of puddle-jumping was for a pair of gumboots. Preferably blue. Maybe with rainbows on them.

Her blue gumboots are waiting, as requested, when Abbie is dropped off for our excursion. The boots fit perfectly and sport a rainbow rocket shooting into outer space. Abbie stomps around the house breaking them in, while demonstrating her puddle-jumping technique. I do a little leap in my own gumboots and hear my right knee creak. This puddle-jumping exercise may require more skill than I realised.

It's a sunny winter's day as we head to the Royal Botanic Garden hoping to find some puddles left from yesterday's rain. We have to walk all the way to Mrs Macquaries Point before we finally spot some shimmering along the footpath near the slipway. Even though the soaring sails of the Sydney Opera House are mere metres away, our eyes are glued only to the ground, investigating the number and depth of puddles at our disposal.

Abbie gives a yelp of delight when she sees one near the sloshing harbour shoreline. She's certain we should try this one first. I ask her how she decides what makes a good puddle. *Well, Didi, it has to be a bit deep so it gives a good splash but not too deep so it gets into your boots.*

Makes perfect sense to me.

She motions me to come and stand next to her, grabs my hand and counts to three. *One... two... three...* and with that we leap into the air, landing a little clumsily (mostly me) in the puddle, sending a spray of water in several arcs around us. We watch as each airborne droplet falls back to earth as liquid sunshine. We giggle and gasp, trying to catch our breath.

That was a good splash, Didi, says Abbie, looking very satisfied as she struts off to find the next puddle to conquer.

I can't move, overwhelmed by the emotion of this simple experience. In this perfect moment under this soaring sky, I want to prescribe puddle-jumping – and Abbie's infectious company – to anyone with a broken heart. *Take a teaspoon of this every day before a meal.*

The next puddle Abbie has found for us is a little higher up on a ledge of sandstone with a more difficult degree of jumpability. Mistime this jump and we could tumble. As we climb over a few boulders to reach it, I ask Abbie why she thinks most adults stop jumping in puddles.

The Secret Life of Puddles

They just don't notice them, she says, shaking her head of blond curls. *They're too busy having boring jobs. Like plumbers. Maybe you don't find your job boring, Didi, but most adults do. They don't play, laugh or smile enough.*

She can't understand why I find what she has said so funny. I guess she's not going to become a plumber.

When we reach our next puddle we discover we are not the first to be drawn to its charms. It's teeming with aquatic life. A perfect shallow crater has formed in the sandstone over time, sculpted by the waves and the wind to create a puddle–rockpool hybrid. It's fringed with tufts of brown and green seaweed and furry mosses. Purple and pink spotted barnacles cling to the rim and tiny sea worms are chugging along the puddle floor. A silver gull hovers over and brazenly joins us on the edge of the rock, dipping and slicing its beak through the water. He fluffs up his neck feathers and dunks his whole head under quickly and then shakes the water off in long, languid flicks as if he's starring in a Decoré shampoo commercial. *We're sure he's putting on a show just for us.*

We don't want to displace this happy colony with a violent splash, so we decide to jump instead in a nearby puddle that is thick and muddy and will test Abbie's new gumboots. This puddle is quite different when we land inside with a stomp. It's viscous and gooey like a mug of chocolate Milo. Quite satisfying is the verdict. Abbie's gumboots have been well christened with a caking of mud that we wash off under a nearby tap.

The Space Between the Stars

She composes a song right on the spot.

Puddles, puddles, puddles,
Jumping in puddles,
Jump, jump, splash
How I love puddles,
Jumping in puddles,
How I love jumping in puddles!

The breeze having picked up a little chill, I wrap up our puddle excursion so I can introduce Abbie to my fig tree on our way back home. As we walk up the slope, our eyes bright and cheeks flushed, Abbie asks me why I call it *my* tree. *Because it speaks to me*, I say matter-of-factly. She nods, accepting this explanation without question.

I want Abbie to love my tree as much as I do, so I'm quietly thrilled when her eyes widen in awe as some of its sweeping branches soon come into view.

It's so big. I bet you can see the whole harbour if you climbed it, she says.

Well why don't you? I ask.

No, I don't think so. I'm too scared. It's too slippery and too high.

I'll help you up if you want. Come on!

She hesitates for a moment, surveying the trunk and the tree's lowest branches, sizing up the difficulty of the task at hand. The promise of a view from up high, that only she will have, helps push down the fear. She runs her fingers over the gnarly trunk and slowly nods her head.

The Secret Life of Puddles

Okay, she says, *I'm going to give it a try.*

I give her a boost. Her footholds are a little perilous, but with a few pushes and lifts from me, she's soon 2 metres up, perched on the first branch, beaming from her accomplishment.

I'm so high! she shouts. *Didi, I can see soooooo far!*

What can you see? I ask.

The harbour, a man jogging, some warships . . . ooooh, and there's a ferry!

Abbie starts crawling among the little hidden hollows between the branches, exploring where she would put her bed and kitchen if she lived there. I tell her that over the years many people have used this tree as shelter, so she wouldn't be the first person to make it a home. This fascinates her and she speculates where they would have slept and where they are now.

She pretends to rummage around near an upper branch she has chosen for her kitchen and hands me down a make-believe cup of tea and slice of orange cake. They are make-believe delicious.

I love this tree, Didi. Can it be our tree?

Of course it can, I say, holding back the tears as I help her back down to earth, where life feels – for the next few hours at least – a little more magical.

CHAPTER 19

Driving

The sun is setting hot and low on the horizon, burning like an out-of-control wildfire. The heat warps the landscape, causing it to buckle and bend like a mirror maze at an amusement park. *Welcome to Africa!*

A herd of giraffe emerges from a gully, already at a gallop, legs like stilts thundering up a dust storm towards our car. The fragility of those long limbs is deceptive. One well-placed kick can shatter a lion's skull or break its spine. They're closing in fast.

We crane our necks out the window as picture-book images come alive right before our eyes. These giraffes seem as tall as skyscrapers as they charge through the golden savannah, dwarfing the stands of mopani and jacaranda trees. The dust from their stampede tastes sweet and peppery. It burns our throat and eyes. There's an unpleasant odour mixed in there too. It's the smell of urine sprayed to mark an animal's territory. It's a warning that we are interlopers and this is no welcoming party.

We all sense the danger without words being exchanged. We've not seen another car in hours on this isolated strip of potholed highway between Gweru and Harare. Even the overcrowded buses, constantly rumbling through Zimbabwe's countryside, know to stay off the road at dusk. There are no streetlights out here to help you avoid animals as they cross to their nearest waterhole. They are not like Tasmania's wildlife. No one's walking away from a head-on with a rhino.

Dad wants to put a bit of distance between us and the giraffes. He steps on the accelerator. Our pale-blue Mini Minor loaded up with five passengers can only muster a cough. *This car is proving a major disappointment.* We were excited when Dad first revealed we were getting a Mini as the family's second car. We'd recently watched the 1969 film *The Italian Job*, which pitted Mini Coopers against police in cheeky chase scenes down stairs, through shopping arcades, between rooftops, across a weir, into the sewer, and even into the back of a moving bus. *These driving feats were what Stargirl was hoping to re-create when our new Mini arrived!*

But the rusty toaster-on-wheels sitting in the driveway when we came home from school was a sorry sight indeed. Rather than having a roguish Michael Caine behind the wheel, this Mini looked like something Basil Fawlty would drive. And now here we are, in the precise situation when a zippy Mini Cooper could get us out of trouble, and all we have as our escape vehicle is this banged-up rust bucket.

There are seven in the giraffe attack herd. Four adults – and three youngsters clearly struggling to keep up with this explosive pace. They are almost parallel with us now – about 200 metres from the road. The rumble of their approach chatters our teeth. It's exhilarating and terrifying at the same time, this car chase across the African plains. Giraffes are supposed to be timid and docile. Why are they in hot pursuit of a decrepit Mini containing a family of five newly arrived Tasmanians?

The waning sun has thrown a paint-spill of rose light across the hills. Shadowy fingers are creeping through the undergrowth with slow menace. We wind up the car windows as the heat begins retreating, preparing for a night of bone-dry cold. Our parents are in two minds about whether to stop and allow the giraffe herd to pass or to continue driving perilously close to this real and present danger. The decision is made to slow down gradually so as not to spook the animals.

It's the worst thing we could have done.

The bull leading the herd immediately does a right-angle turn and begins galloping directly towards us, his eyes as black as coal. Stargirl lets out a squeak of terror as we feel the road shake beneath us. Dreamcatcher starts whimpering and I brace for impact, shielding my eyes with my hands, unable to picture what a giraffe attack could possibly look like. Will we be stomped to death or torn to shreds by those huge teeth?

And then, as the moment of impact is upon us, a stillness descends as if we've been trapped in a bubble containing all the time in the world.

I open my eyes to see four hooves soar just behind the car like a thoroughbred stallion making a jump in an equestrian event. But the degree of difficulty of this vault is far superior. This giraffe is jumping to avoid a moving obstacle. He lands on the other side of the road in a thud of dust, legs spread-eagled to take the impact. How Dad has kept a steady hand on the wheel, powering on, I'll never understand. Even Michael Caine would have broken out in a sweat.

As we look back through the rear window, we can see the giraffe's nostrils snorting from exertion, and what's that look in his eyes? Satisfaction? Victory? He may not be classed as one of the Big Five game animals, but a giraffe bull should never be underestimated. The rest of his herd soon joins him, rubbing their cheeks against his long muscular neck, celebrating his Olympian feat.

As we leave the clearing and the giraffes disappear from sight, our eyes are still as wide as saucers. Is this what living in Africa is going to be like? An *Indiana Jones* adventure at every turn? *And we thought a lack of laws requiring us to wear seatbelts was going to be the thrill.*

The rest of the journey is disappointingly dreary in comparison. Besides an unexpected buffalo roadblock that adds an hour to our return trip home, the rest of our weekend away visiting some distant relatives is as dull as dishwater.

The Mini's encounter with the giraffe has excited Stargirl like nothing else. The car has become a magical portal, a flying carpet from the *Arabian Nights* that can transport her to an amazing world where giraffes leap over cars.

She demands to sit in the front seat next to Dad whenever possible so she can watch how he changes gears and rides the clutch. Even though she is only twelve years old, her fascination with driving becomes an obsession. Most days before school she heads up to the hill behind the house where the Mini is garaged and sits in the driver's seat re-creating imaginary car chases and rally tours. *Baking heat, dust clouds, mud sprays, wheel spins, crowds cheering, champagne corks, winner's podium. Stargirl and the Mini pitted against the world.*

Even though Dreamcatcher and I are older siblings, we have no doubt Stargirl will be the first to get her driver's licence and then buy a car. It is all she can talk about. She becomes a curiosity among the adults, able to talk makes and models like a cigar-chomping car dealer.

One morning as we are preparing for school there's an almighty crash of metal grinding against concrete. It comes from the direction of the garage. One by one we race up the driveway to the hill to see the Mini's back bumper bar embedded in the garage wall. In the front seat looking sheepish is Stargirl.

It transpires that for the past three weeks, in the early hours of the morning, Stargirl has been secretly taking the Mini on short test drives up and down the back driveway. Unbeknown to anyone she has been expertly changing gears, braking and steering the Mini around the garbage bins. What's brought her a cropper this time is attempting to reverse park with one of the garage doors closed. When we find her, she is propped up on two pillows with the driver's seat pushed up right against the steering wheel so she can reach the pedals.

Parental fury hits a scale never seen before. *They are apoplectic.* Even Stargirl seems to understand that her cute dimpled smile isn't going to save her this time. She is yanked out of the car and marched back to the house, where a two-pronged reprimand ensues. The tirade ends quickly when our parents realise how shaken she is by her own actions.

The Mini is never repaired after the accident. We will be moving back to Australia soon; it isn't worth the trouble. As it putters around the streets of Gweru, ferrying us around, its mangled bumper bar is a permanent reminder of the day Stargirl went too far. The day Stargirl went too far before this final time.

Her passion for driving and cars broke in her that day. Although she later registered for her learner's permit and had a few lessons, she never did get her driver's licence. A driver's licence is a rite of passage for most teenagers. Your first real test in the adult world. Your ticket

Driving

to freedom and independence. As more years passed, Stargirl's decision not to possess one was as much a statement of her rebellious nature as anything else. *I can drive a car. I don't need a plastic card to prove it.*

She was accomplished in so many ways, but despite all her achievements, holding a driver's licence was one of the few things that eluded her. The headstrong girl who was driving at the age of twelve chose to be a passenger instead.

It was the only area of her life where she let someone else get behind the wheel.

CHAPTER 20

High as a Kite

It's 4.30 am. This is my favourite time to write. Banging away at my keyboard in the almost-morning when Mark is asleep in the other room and the city is yet to stir. When I have only the wind for company.

I can't see the wind but I know it is there. I can see how it plays. How it whistles through the seal of my balcony window, turning the wooden blinds into a vertical xylophone, how it quivers through the winter seedlings I've just planted in a row of pots, or how it skates across the moonshine mirrored on the harbour.

It must be fun to be the wind, to dip and dive and rumble and roar or just disappear quietly without a whisper. I've been watching the wind more closely these past few months. Of all the forces of nature, it's the most elusive, always in hiding, only its actions giving away its presence. Which is why, for my next immersive urban nature adventure, I want to harness those powers.

I'm planning to do something I haven't done since I was ten years old. I'm going to fly a kite. And I'm going to do it with Michael Richards, who knows a thing or two about kites – and the wind.

Michael and I are meeting just a few hundred metres from my fig tree, outside the Art Gallery in the Domain. The lawns are buzzing with crowds arriving to see the finalists of this year's Archibald Prize for portraiture. At this time of year, I would normally be with them, in the dim light, doing a crab shuffle from portrait to portrait, intently examining the walls of famous faces.

Yet these days indoors holds so little appeal. I want to shout to the throng – *Hey! Hang out with me instead! I have a date with the wind!* My re-enchantment with nature has rekindled my inner child. I can't wait to scamper through the grass, under the sun, squinting into the wide blue sky, tethered to a long-tailed comet. I can feel the joy rising just thinking about it.

Michael arrives carrying a long canvas bag big enough to fit a canoe. *What's he got in there? A kite that size could take us to the moon.* With his gentle weathered features under his battered hat, and his khaki attire, Michael could have walked out of a verse of 'Waltzing Matilda'. People often use the phrase *He walks with a spring in his step* – well, Michael is one of those people who truly does. He's a human pogo stick. As we bounce down the hill towards the Domain, he tells me he also teaches juggling and unicycling. I picture him living with his family under a Big Top, all wearing rainbow-coloured wigs and carrying Harpo Marx horns. I smile. Michael's inner child would never be far from the surface.

Michael has been teaching people to fly kites for thirty years. In fact, seven years ago Michael and a group of his mates broke the world record for the highest-altitude kite flight. Their base camp was an isolated sheep station in outback New South Wales so they wouldn't disrupt flight paths. Their determination was impressive: after forty attempts over ten years they finally cracked it, sending their kite an extraordinary 5 kilometres into the earth's atmosphere. *Five kilometres! I'll be happy just to get my kite off the ground.* I feel a flutter of performance anxiety.

The Domain will make a perfect launch pad for my maiden lift-off – a large field of open grass, trees faraway on the fence line, with no powerlines or obstructions. I'm concerned there's only a kiss of a breeze, but Michael assures me the wind will appear when we need it. It blows differently this time of the year, here, near the Royal Botanic Garden. It tends to come off the water and change direction quickly. I'll have to keep my wits about me.

Michael unzips his bag of assorted contraptions and pulls out a packet. It contains the kit for the first kite I'm going to flight-test. It's a design similar to the ones from my childhood – a diamond shape with a long tail. It has a texture like paper but Michael explains it's made from Tyvek – a polyethylene fabric that's lightweight, durable and waterproof.

Michael encourages me to personalise it, so I draw a rough picture of my fig tree on it for good luck. I tape down the two fibreglass rods in a cross on the back and then thread through some string attached to a spindle. The final touch – tying two long, blue and red shimmering ribbons to its bottom point that will act as a tail, giving the kite drag and balance.

My flying machine is ready.

We stride out into the middle of the field, following in the footsteps of all the great aviators who have gone before us. Michael holds up my kite and asks me to walk a few metres to the west away from him and then to give a tug on the string. The breeze is much stronger here surprisingly. Little gusts are swirling around my head, tossing my fringe in my eyes.

I follow Michael's instructions and watch as my kite gently lifts into the air as if powered by magic. It hovers there for a bit until I release more string, and then it's like taking a dog for a walk in the sky. The kite yanks at its tether, demanding more slack as it veers left then right, climbing higher and higher.

I start giggling inexplicably as sunlight bounces off the trail of shiny ribbons. Something as simple as watching this little kite dart and loop in the breeze is filling me with a giddy delight. It's as though the kite is an extension of my body and my hand can touch the sky. It's as close as I can get to being airborne myself.

Michael is enjoying my reaction. He says I have the hugest smile on my face. It's why he enjoys teaching so much. And the teachers in his school groups get just as affected as the kids. His Kite Magic company in the Sydney beachside suburb of Coogee supplies kites for all types of recreational and club activities, although increasingly Michael is being asked to use kite-flying to help students better engage with science and nature. He sees kids who struggle in the classroom come out of their shell during a kite session. They relish being freed from their four-walled enclosures and engaging in a battle of wits with the wind.

The enchantment of a kite is that it pulls you into a new focus. It takes you to the *periphery of your ordinary attention*, as biologist E.O. Wilson so perfectly describes it. There is no room in your head for worry or anxiety or rumination. You're completely engrossed in the moment and the pressing task at hand – keeping your kite airborne. At times it can require the utmost concentration, tugging at the string when the wind dips, releasing more slack as it picks up again, scooting a few steps here and then doubling back just as quickly. And then, in the next instant, nothing much is required from you at all other than just holding on and letting the current you've captured do all the work.

Michael wants me to try another kite. He rummages about in his bag of tricks, retrieves an assortment of fabric and wooden frames, and begins expertly assembling our next flying machine. It's a rectangular box kite, about a metre long, as aqua blue as the sky.

I have barely time to hold on to the spindle as the kite shoots up into the sky like a thoroughbred blasting out of the stalls. *Whoaaaaa!* It flies like a dream, sprinting through the air, the kite's fabric as taut as muscle. I need to keep a firmer grip on the spindle. *This filly has real spirit!*

My box kite's simple appearance belies her aerodynamic strength. In fact, near Wollongong on the South Coast, just 85 kilometres from where I'm standing, a distant relative of this box kite made aviation history. Its inventor, Lawrence Hargrave (the chap on Australia's original $20 note), strapped himself to four of these box kites and became the first Australian to fly. *Wouldn't I love my own Mary Poppins moment right now.*

Several office workers cutting through the park on their lunchbreak stop and point at my kite, clearly captivated. If only they could see the delight on their faces they would skip work and play with us instead. Two older Chinese women pushing a friend in a wheelchair are also entranced and pause to watch. I want to give them a good show but I've let out too much string and it is knotting around my feet. My grip flounders and my kite begins descending in a fast spiral. Despite my panicked zigzagging the breeze eludes me. The Chinese women shout at me to move back quickly and to yank the string hard. I follow their instructions and my kite comes alive, swooping skyward again in a swirl of ribbon. Crashlanding averted. My spectators approve and give some admiring cheers.

High as a Kite

Michael isn't surprised by the interaction. He says that unlike in Australia, kite-flying in China is largely an adult activity, with hundreds of people participating in festivals through the year. I can now see why kite-flying would be appealing for those looking for outdoor exercise with another dimension.

The wind has found playmates elsewhere and the box kite gently falls to the ground despite my resuscitation attempts. Michael has another class to teach, so I reluctantly help him fold up the kites before we head back to his car. I thank him for the gift he's shared with me and the joy it has rekindled. He promises to pop another beginners' kite in the mail so I can take Abbie kite-flying with me next time.

Streams of animated art viewers are leaving the Art Gallery as I cut through the grounds to Woolloomooloo. They chatter to their friends about their favourite Archibald portraits and which one they think will take out the top prize. Their smiles are still not enough to entice me inside. After my morning of kite-flying there's a new skip in my step.

Flying kites is all about finding the right balance. It's the art of knowing when to hold on and when to let go – something I've been struggling with since Stargirl's death. To be a successful kite-flyer is to be in a waltz with the wind, you and your dance partner drawing on each other's strength, supporting one moment and then allowing yourself to be carried the next. I'm not very good at allowing others to carry me. Too accustomed to being the big sister, the school prefect. As I flew my kites, I could see how I held the string too tightly, not letting the wind do some of the work. Another metaphor for my life perhaps.

You're always going to lose if you try to fight the wind. Surrender yourself to its currents and, like a kite, it will propel you forward.

CHAPTER 21

Fortieth and Surprise Wedding

I rap the brass doorknocker three times (*there it is again, that magic number three*). Mark and I hear the thundering of little feet running down the hallway towards the front door. The metal letterbox flap creaks open and a pair of large brown eyes peeps through. *They're here!* squeals Stargirl's young daughter, Stormtrooper, as she wrestles with the chain latch and doorknob. We hear another set of approaching footsteps – this time an adult's – and then Stargirl's partner, Dances With Wolves, is swinging open the door with a big welcoming grin, dishcloth in hand. We exchange kisses and hugs, then they usher us into the lounge to offer us wine and an elegant cheese plate to graze through.

A sprinkling of friends and family is already milling around in the back garden, chatting excitedly, as the winter dusk filters through the bare branches of the birch tree. It looks magical out there. Fairy lights have been strung along the fence, and the new hardwood deck – fast-tracked for Stargirl's fortieth birthday party tonight – glistens from a recent coat of varnish.

We spot Mum, Dreamcatcher and Dreamcatcher's family near the cubbyhouse and head over to say hello. There have been some family tensions. Dad and his new family are absent. It's been months since Dreamcatcher and I have seen each other. Now that the three of us live in three different states – me in Sydney, Dreamcatcher in Adelaide and Stargirl in Melbourne – time together is usually a quick dinner squeezed between interstate work commitments. Neither of us has seen Stargirl since last Christmas. Dreamcatcher and I have been concerned. Our younger sister has been distant and cagey.

Dreamcatcher and I pull away from the rest of the family, and slip into an easy sisterly download of all the recent happenings. I fill her in on what my adult stepchildren are up to and how quickly our grandson is growing up, with another grandchild on the way. She tells me about her son's success on the footy field, her teenage daughter's recent trip away and her never-finished bathroom renovation.

And then, as if from nowhere, shyly shimmying towards us is Stargirl, sheathed in a green, mid-thigh slip dress, teeth flashing in a big smile for her big sisters. She is a vision of exquisiteness. Radiant. *This is how*

Fortieth and Surprise Wedding

I always want to remember her. She gives us each a kiss on the cheek, leaving her usual calling card – a smudge of burgundy-red lipstick. We can smell the tobacco on her breath. She's been behind the house smoking with two colleagues. They're hanging back just behind her looking sheepish. Maybe they've had some weed as well. There isn't a drug Stargirl hasn't experimented with. She's told us some. The rest we've guessed. Over the years, she's sometimes arrived late at a dinner or drinks with a new boyfriend in tow – one of them once known in our circles as a heroin user. We suspect she is dabbling in that as well. She's used acid and coke and meth and amphetamines, but her preferred self-medication is alcohol. A cigarette in one hand, a glass of wine in the other. *The legal drugs that can be just as lethal.*

Stargirl's propensity for high-risk behaviour went into overdrive when we were teenagers – around the time our parents divorced and built new lives with new partners. The naughty imps that had circled her since childhood now found a foothold as demons. Her brilliant mind began fracturing. She struggled with the demands of study and then the daily deadlines of her career in print journalism. Drugs became her crutch.

Soon she was a media adviser to the Victorian premier, drafting press releases and fielding media enquiries with aplomb. And all the while she kept ignoring her underlying mental health struggles. There were many bouts of darkness, depression and mania. We suspected she was bipolar.

We managed to get her to a psychiatrist once, and a few counsellors, but she always ignored their advice and recovery regime. At least back then there were more good days than bad. And in a media and political world of high-functioning alcoholics and drug users, Stargirl's problems didn't stand out. *She'd found the perfect place to hide in full view.*

There's a flash from someone's camera and I'm back among the twinkling lights of the garden. Guests are being encouraged to gather around the deck for celebratory speeches and toasts. Stargirl is beaming. She's never looked happier. Meeting Dances With Wolves and having Stormtrooper has settled her into herself, made her seem less flighty and furtive. I'm hoping she'll get the help she needs now that she has a family to live for.

After a birthday speech from her best friend, a woman steps between Stargirl and Dances With Wolves and announces that she is a celebrant who has been asked to marry them tonight. A surprise wedding as well as a birthday! A cheer rolls through the guests as we realise the extra specialness of this night. My heart aches for many things in this moment, but mostly I pray that the fierceness of their passion will help Stargirl love herself again.

After vows are exchanged, Stormtrooper is given the job of handing over the wedding bands to the celebrant. Her chubby fingers fumble and one of the rings falls, almost slipping through a gap in the new decking boards.

There is a collective gasp from the crowd. Tragedy averted. The ring is retrieved and the wedding rites are completed. *Husband and wife.* To seal the union, Stargirl and Dances With Wolves kiss long and deeply, blissfully unaware of the audience witnessing this intense moment of intimacy.

What would we have said then had we known that despite this perfect bond of love and hope, their lives would be shattered in the cruellest of ways, one of them farewelling the other in a coffin long before they had a chance to grow old together? Now, as I type these words, it's still so painful for my heart to revisit that evening. *Wretchedly tragic is how the great romantic fatalists would describe it.* How else to explain the hand that fate would deal?

There was Stargirl, in her back garden, basking in the adoration of her new husband, tiny daughter by her side, surrounded by a golden circle of family and friends, just a few metres from where she would take her life eight years later.

CHAPTER 22

Ants in Your Pants

The morning shadows are playing tricks in this broken light.

From my grassy knoll, the bumpy ridges running along the trunk of my tree look as wide and deep as canyons. There are soaring cliffs plummeting to weathered riverbeds. The bark is as dense as eroded rock. There are mountain ranges of peaks and ledges, summits that defy gravity and below them ravines that plunge into an unknown abyss.

After watching this light-play conjure inches into miles I need to convince myself that it has indeed been a trick of the eye. I walk across and run my fingers over the barky contours for myself. And yes, when I'm standing up close there are no grand canyons embedded here. *Just miniature ones.*

I close my eyes and use my fingertips to read the bark like braille. The knots and bumps feel smoother than they look. What would they say if I could decipher the code? I almost expect to feel a heartbeat through this knobbly skin, the life force is so singular and robust. I reach deep into its being. It's not a beat; rather a flow, a systolic swoosh in and out like the soft purring of a cat. My own heartbeat slows to match it.

It's getting stronger, my heart. I can feel it repairing the tears and gashes, applying soothing balms to the cuts and bruises, making itself heal. *I can see a way out.*

I feel something crawl on my hand and open my eyes to see several ants, in single file, making their way across my thumb. Their tiny feet and antennae tickle my skin as they scale my nails and knuckles and make their way across what – to them – must feel like the Himalayas. These mighty mountaineers are part of a wider ecosystem that relies on my tree as much as I do. There are rich pickings here for an ant colony. There's milky sap to harvest, pollen, decaying leaf litter and decomposing insects.

My walk with a man who loves ants has given me a fascinating window into the lives of these tiny critters – so much so that every time I plant a footstep now, I'm painfully aware of the genocide I'm committing. My 'ant man', Ajay Narendra, nods with understanding when I tell him this. *It happens to many people once they become aware of ants,* he says.

I tracked Ajay down at Sydney's Macquarie University, after reading one of his articles about the extraordinary navigational abilities of ants. Ajay's macroscopic photos of these foot soldiers were mesmerising in their beauty and detail. This was a man whose love of nature had given him an ant's view of the world. *Make yourself small not big. Set your goals and then surrender to them.*

We arrange to meet in the Domain on an overcast day. Ajay has a softness about him and large playful brown eyes. I can imagine him becoming so absorbed with his insect protégés that he would miss mealtimes and appointments regularly.

We're barely 2 metres into our ant excursion before we're both crouching on the footpath, peering at a small, seemingly innocuous mound of dirt between two pavers. It's a little ant nest, Ajay tells me, possibly supporting a colony of about 100 meat ants, the most dominant ant species in Australia. They're expert colonisers and you find them everywhere – except for Tasmania. It's still a little chilly for them (ants hate the cold), so there's no sign of any inhabitants yet. But when the sun warms up they'll be swarming . . . well . . . *like ants.*

The grey clouds are lifting as we continue our ant hunt to the Royal Botanic Garden. There are dozens of meat-ant mounds to be found now that I know what to look for. Some are showing signs of life, with several residents poking their heads up, antennae twitching to take the temperature of the day.

Ajay has the same infectious wonder I've seen in all my nature guides. He was educated in Bangalore in India, and it was while hiking as a child in the forests surrounding his home that he first became enamoured of the world of insects. He studied environmental science and chemistry, and then did his honours and a PhD in entomology. *He'd caught the bug, so to speak.*

He found his way to Sydney just over a decade ago because he fell in love with Australia's ants. *They're simply beautiful,* he says, lighting up with genuine reverence. He becomes more animated as he describes their sheer variation in structure. I'd always thought most ants looked alike. Far from it. Some have large eyes, some have small ones. Some have eyes in the front – others have eyes towards the back of their head. Their mandibles or jaws can vary greatly as well.

As we reach the building works surrounding the Art Gallery's new extension, our ant quest gets a little more exciting. The sun is slowly heating up the ground, enticing a myriad of ants out of their homes. Hundreds of black specs are milling about with great urgency. In fact, urgency seems to be an ant's default setting. It's possibly all that formic acid they're filled with.

Despite their reputation for aggression, ants are quite altruistic, Ajay explains. It's a genetic strength that allows them to live in vast colonies in a highly efficient manner. Unlike humans, who share just 50 per cent of the same genes with their siblings, worker ant sisters share 75 per cent of their genes – their similarity to each other ensuring a selfless, harmonious approach to life in the collective.

Ajay says that we could encounter about 30–35 different species of ants just along my regular walk. Some are *arboreal* – in the trees – others are subterranean species that forage largely underground, and the rest are the meat ants whose nests can spread for metres. It's the generalists that thrive in the inner city. They're less fussy eaters that can feed on whatever is around, from sugary leftovers to bird droppings, which are valued for their high nitrogen content.

As we head past the Andrew (Boy) Charlton Pool, we pass a long trail of ants marching up a tree with purpose. I have the human urge to block their path with my hand to see what they will do but I stop myself, not wanting to disturb their focus.

Ajay notices my deepening awareness. He says that often when he takes people on ant walks, they are – as humans often are – oblivious to the many creatures with which they share their world. Children who come with their parents sometimes start stomping on the ants and their nests as Ajay points them out. Their wantonness can sometimes break his heart, but it is difficult to admonish other people's children. What he tries to do – as he does with his own son – is to educate them and introduce them to being in awe of these little creatures and the important work they do in the cycle of decomposition and renewal.

Ajay's suburban ant walks were very popular before lockdowns. A typical two-hour ant walk is usually across a 2-kilometre stretch, but sometimes the group doesn't even leave the carpark because there is so much ant activity to investigate there. Interest in Ajay's excursions comes mostly from gardeners who want to manage their backyard ants without using harmful pesticides. There are also growing numbers of school-age children joining Ajay's expeditions who are keen to know more after seeing a nature documentary.

Ajay says there's no better place than Australia to study ants. Australia has more of them than anywhere else – some 1500 species. It's partly to do with our climate and landscape, with its large tracts of arid and semi-arid land in which ants thrive.

As we hike up the hill to my tree, it's as if I've slipped on a pair of ant goggles. I start to see everything crawling with ants – blades of grass, leaves, tree trunks, bush rock. How could I have been so oblivious to this ant metropolis before?

When we reach the clearing near my tree, we pause, eyes focused on the ground for any movement, and sure enough there are several busy zones of ants. And they're all so different. Large ones, small ones, orange ones. Ajay explains that most ants only forage 20–30 centimetres away from their nest. Others, like the bull ant, can travel as far as 25 metres in search of a feed for its colony. That's a long way to go on tiny legs. And the hauls they carry! Up to fifty times their body weight. As Ralph Waldo Emerson saluted in his *Nature* essay, that's *a little body with a mighty heart*.

In this context, my own problems pale in comparison to the average exhausting day of these tireless workers. Especially since their life span is so short – just seven to eight days.

And I feel robbed that I only had forty-eight years with Stargirl.

How precious every moment would feel if we injected our years with the gratitude of ants. What would I do if I knew I only had a week to live like an ant does? How do I know I don't? *If an ant can find purpose in such a short existence, have I been squandering mine?*

We've seen little aggression displayed among the different ant colonies. Ajay says while ants are territorial, and there are some fearsome ones invading our shores – like the Argentine ants and the yellow crazy ants – generally ants tend to keep to their own patch. And on the rare occasion they do need to defend their ground, they can exhibit some unusual behaviour.

Instead of hand-to-hand combat, meat ants, for example, perform a choreographed dance to fend off intruders. They stand on their tiptoes like dainty ballerinas and punch like kickboxers, spinning and twirling as they go. No wonder trespassers get confused and hurry away. Ajay says it's mesmerising to watch these exquisite routines, which have evolved in order to avoid death from warfare. Another sensible lesson we can take from ants.

Our ant safari complete, we head back to Potts Point through the commuter throng, Ajay regaling me, as we walk, with more amazing ant facts . . . *Did you know ants don't have ears? . . . they don't have lungs either . . . And they have two stomachs . . .*

I'm still thinking of those dancing ants. They remind me of Stargirl and her love of dancing. When she shimmied and swayed, captivating us all with her lithe, sinuous body, was she actually performing her version of a war dance? Were her twists and thrusts part of an exhausting choreography to ward off the demons that haunted her?

Was that why she made the music stop?

CHAPTER 23

Uber Goodbye

I'm not sure how long I've been on autopilot. Fragments of memory swirl around, caught in the wintery gusts of my mind ... the hearse leaving the funeral home, the utterly distraught faces of Dances With Wolves and Stormtrooper, their little dog Harry with his sorrowful eyes, consoling hugs, weak cups of hot tea. Not being able to breathe.

To magnify the grief, Stormtrooper turns twelve the day after the funeral. I've offered to bake her a birthday cake as her mum always did. I inspect the cupboards of our Melbourne Airbnb. They are stocked with a few dented trays I hope I can fashion into cake tins. I can't work the timer, and the dizzying array of settings on the oven make no sense at all. Hopefully the party guests will be forgiving.

I flick through images on my phone and decide on a chocolate fort cake, inspired by one from the *Women's*

Weekly Children's Birthday Cake cookbook. Mounds of whipped chocolate butter icing covered in smarties, surrounded by a fence of chocolate finger biscuits. It will be an important symbol of normality, of continuity, of life carrying on even when you no longer have a mother. *Who am I kidding – how can any cake carry that sort of burden?* As if it knows the enormity of the expectation at hand, the cake sinks in the middle as it comes out of the oven and I have to cover the depression with extra icing.

Melbourne is deep in its first long Covid lockdown, so friends and cousins arrive in socially distanced numbers. We are thankful for the children and the dogs able to be just children and dogs. All we adults can do is clutch at our wine glasses, peering deeply into their contents as if they are crystal balls that can foresee the future.

Mark and I have a long surreal drive back through Victoria. Town after town deserted. Pubs empty, restaurants shuttered up, hotels operating with a skeleton staff we never see. We crave country-town comfort and kindness after our harrowing two weeks, but instead we are treated like aliens, virus carriers, people to fear. *It's only human.*

Returning so soon to host my ABC weekend late-night radio show is possibly akin to madness. I have been offered as much time as I need, but how can I take off *the rest of my life?* My radio studio is my chocolate cake. Evidence that normal carries on somewhere else. That there is something useful I can do. Headphones, mic, screens, buttons and faders, on-air light . . . *Welcome to Nightlife . . . thanks for joining me . . .*

I overestimate the resilience of some of my listeners as the unknowingness of lockdown stretches into an abyss. The darkness brings out their demons and then my own. *Why is this happening? When will it end? Who can we blame?* All the same questions I asked when Stargirl died.

Listeners in Melbourne are at breaking point. Endless days of isolation are sending their anxiety through the roof. They demand constant virus updates, more sympathy – while listeners in Perth, which has largely escaped outbreaks, want the depressing talk of death and disease to moderate so they can enjoy their escape to the beach. It's challenging to find the right balance on a national radio show with an audience scattered across borders. In a letter published in *The Age* I'm accused of being insensitive, of not understanding how traumatic lockdown in Melbourne is because I do not live there. The unfairness of this criticism stings. I want to say I know some of the trauma all too well.

Of course, I do not say this at the time. We broadcasters are emergency workers, doing our job by helping keep everyone informed and safe, knowing we'll often interact with people on the worst day of their life. Sometimes on the worse day of *our* life. My studio producer, Dave Prior, deserves a medal for fielding calls, calming and reassuring, being a friend to the inconsolable. Keeping people on the line until a Lifeline counsellor is available.

In the radio biz, overnight work is referred to as the 'graveyard shift' due to the unsocial hours. This first weekend of broadcasts after Stargirl's death has given the phrase added poignancy. When the on-air light goes off in the early hours of Monday morning, I feel the accumulated exhaustion of the last few weeks. I'm like a balloon deflating.

The night offers no reprieve. As I stagger out of the studio to meet my Uber, the cold wet air sucks at my bones. It is 2.09 am when I check my phone to see how far away my ride is. I notice the date. It has ticked over to Monday, 8 June. My stomach churns as the significance of those numbers registers. Today would have been Stargirl's forty-ninth birthday. I knew this anniversary was approaching but I hadn't planned to be standing here on a deserted street in the drizzling gloom, marking it alone.

A new wave of grief is just beginning to rise when a red Ford Fiesta rumbles into the ABC Ultimo driveway. Its appearance doesn't fill me with confidence. There's a huge dent on the front passenger side, flaking rust around the wheel rims and a missing hub cap. I consider cancelling my booking and ordering another car, but then, feeling the wind pick up, decide against it. This bomb will have to be my uncomfortable ride home while I try to keep my insides *inside.*

Uber Goodbye

Sightly frazzled, I open the back door and start loading in my work bags, laptop and microphone. My notebook and drink bottle spill out. I curse under my breath, picking them up and hastily throwing them onto the back seat.

Take your time, says the driver, sensing my anxiety.

His warmth takes me aback. He has a soothing sing-song voice with a distinctive southern African accent I recognise instantly. It's unusual to meet an Uber driver here in Sydney from my home region of Africa. I'm curious but can't make out his features because he is as dark as the night. He must be tall though, because his knees are almost touching the steering wheel.

I close the door and fasten my seatbelt. That's when I notice the track on the radio. It's 'Africa' by Toto, Stargirl's favourite song. The coincidence takes my breath away. I'm immediately transported to a school social in Zimbabwe, where we danced wildly to this song after stealing our first taste of local moonshine beer. Stargirl was hypnotising as she swayed and writhed, the music moving through her veins like liquid gold. This song cannot be a coincidence. The memory is too specific. Too intimate.

Where are we going? the driver asks me, dragging me back to the present. This is a very odd question since he should already have the address programmed into his GPS system. I should be concerned by his amateurish-ness and inexperience. Strangely I'm not. Even though

I'm exhausted from using my voice all night, I tell him not to worry and that I will give him street-by-street directions as we go.

Relieved, he flashes a brilliant white smile in the rear-vision mirror and pulls out of the driveway into Harris Street. *There's something so familiar about that smile.* My initial apprehension is dissipating. I feel unexpectedly safe with this stranger. There's a gentleness and childlike innocence about him. He feels like a younger brother. I sense he trusts me as well.

We turn onto Broadway. Covid and the weather have emptied the streets. There isn't a soul to be seen in this usually busy late-night quarter – besides a solitary food-delivery cyclist battling through the downpour. The windscreen wipers whine and screech as the rain gets heavier.

Have you finished work? he asks, in his rich warm voice.

Yes, I have, I say. *It's been a tough week. Looking forward to some days off. Have you got more jobs after this?*

No, he says, another big smile forming. *This is my last job. I am then going to a friend's house to have a drink – you see, it's my birthday today.*

He takes his eyes off the road and looks at me in the rear-vision mirror as if to monitor my reaction. I hope he can't see the shock on my face.

Happy birthday, I say, struggling to form the words.

This cannot be possible.

Uber Goodbye

Suddenly I'm thrown back into my seat, as his knees knock the steering wheel and we lurch into the next lane. He quickly corrects the car and we swerve into the Cross City Tunnel, heading to the Eastern Suburbs. *He really is a hopeless driver.*

So this man who has picked me up in his Uber has the same birthday as Stargirl. Life throws up many random connections but this one feels eerie and otherworldly. Do I put it down to coincidence and leave it at that, or do I dare ask a follow-up question that is almost certain to make this one of the most extraordinary encounters of my life?

I try to sound as casual as possible. *So, how old are you today?*

There's a slight pause before he answers. It feels like an eternity. *I'm forty-nine years old.*

Even though this was the answer I was quietly hoping for, my throat catches as I inhale a deep breath all the way from the beginning of time.

This cannot be happening.

I want to tell him today is also my sister's birthday and then, not wanting to break the magic spell, decide against it.

My mind is racing through all the possible explanations for these twists of fate. The most likely one is too inconceivable to consider. I look out the window and watch the lights on the walls of the tunnel flash by like exploding rockets. My broken heart wants to soar and laugh and dance and rip itself out of my body so it can fly out of its cage. *Not yet. I need to know more.*

I ask him where he is from, as he misjudges the roundabout on Elizabeth Bay Road and mounts the concrete perimeter, rattling the remaining wheel caps.

I was born in South Africa, he says.

I tell him I was also born in South Africa, in Pietermaritzburg.

But I am half Zimbabwean. My mother is from Bulawayo and I grew up there, he says.

The coincidences have stopped amazing me. It's as if I know the answers before I ask the questions.

We also grew up in Zimbabwe, in Gweru, I say.

He just nods as if he already knows this too.

As we make a wild turn into Macleay Street he starts talking about the terrible leaders Africa is blighted with and how the African people deserve better. *The African disease,* he says, using the same phrase Stargirl would often use when we discussed the politics of Africa.

I say what I always said to her: *There are bad leaders all over the world. Not just in Africa.*

He shakes his head like an old man who has seen it all before. No one likes to see their own people suffer.

We pull up outside my apartment building under a streetlight. For the first time I can see his face clearly. He has smooth ebony skin – much younger than his forty-nine years – dreadlocks and a face glowing with such ethereal joy and serenity I know I have been driven home by an angel.

Here we are, he says proudly, even surprising himself that he's managed to get me home in one piece.

I thank him and he turns around ever so slowly, as if to put as much meaning as he can summon into what he is about to utter. *Goodbye,* he says and flashes me a smile I know instantly.

It belongs to Stargirl. My beautiful Stargirl. The same mouth, the same lips, the same teeth.

I don't want to get out of the car. I don't want to leave her.

I want to ask, *How are you? Where did you go? Why did you leave?* But the questions do not come because there are no answers.

She has come back to say goodbye. That is all I need to know.

She wanted to drive me for a change. Something she never got to do when she was here before. As the big sister I always led – as the little sister she always followed. Tonight, she is where she needs to be. Behind the wheel. Even though it was her birthday, Stargirl wanted to give *me* a gift. She wanted to take me on a joy-ride.

As I watch her banged-up little red car disappear along Macleay Street, I feel a supernatural elation – as if I'm levitating. My head is bursting with clarity. Stargirl needed to leave this place. I know this now. She is a time traveller on a long celestial journey. She stayed with us as long as she could.

In bed, ready for my first good sleep in months, I look out onto the city, at my fig tree softly framed in the moonlight, solid and certain. I couldn't have wished for a better spirit guide during these past months. It has stood true and constant.

For the first time in a long time I don't feel lost any more. The light from Stargirl is warming me from within.

Travel safely, Mooks.

Dust to Dust

I began writing this book thinking that by its end I might solve the whydunnit – why a brilliant, beautiful woman would leave behind Dances With Wolves and Stormtrooper and her magnificent life. As I approach the last pages, I am no closer to understanding why this happened than I was at the start. Although I am nearer to finding my own peace with it.

Stargirl's mental health was deteriorating. This much we know. She could no longer work or engage with the outside world. She was in extreme emotional anguish. But this explains only part of why she could not bear to go on. She was surrounded by family and professional support. The help was there if she had only taken the next step. To her, for some reason, that step loomed like a chasm. Even with all the love in the world she slipped through our fingers.

Ernest Hemingway's advice was to *Write hard and clear about what hurts,* and that is what I have been doing these past months – writing away the pain as I explore the catacombs of my own despair. Buried deep within these caves of grief, I've chipped away at the sediment bit by bit, to uncover what lies beneath.

What I have found has, at times, paralysed me with its horror. I understand now why we keep things buried in our bag of shadows, afraid to look inside. But what we fear is worse than what we find.

I have learned this bravery from nature.

The stoicism of my tree is surpassed only by its generosity. No matter how many creatures it feeds and protects there is always room for me. I will never be turned away while it is anchored to that stony hillside.

My little urban patch of green has become my whole world. At first it was due to limitation and reduction. Now it is by choice. I have no need for much more than this. My backyard is the universe. The sun, wind and clouds have become my constant companions, keeping me buoyant and playful even when my feet have, at times, felt as heavy as clay. And if a tiny weed can find nourishment in a spartan crack in a footpath, surely there are sufficient riches here for me.

Allowing myself to rest and retreat in this glint of green has replaced the rumination with revelry. There are just so many more interesting things going on out here in the natural world than inside my head. A march of Lilliputian ants ferrying leaf litter back and forth from their nest becomes my own *Gulliver's Travels*. They live with such purpose and camaraderie. They show me how joy can be harnessed from debris and spun into gold. Trash can be a poor man's truffles. A loss doesn't mean the end.

Stargirl's life force is now part of this world. She is there in the earth beneath my feet. When I feel a breeze on my cheek, that is her breath. When the morning sun warms my face, it is her embrace.

And when the light from the furthest star in the furthest galaxy flickers in the night sky, I know it is a kiss goodnight from her.

Acknowledgements

I've always felt as though *The Space Between the Stars* existed even before I came along. Have other writers felt this? Maybe so. My only job has been to distil its essence onto the page. Easier said than done, of course. Writing a book about your younger sister's suicide while you're in and out of pandemic lockdowns wouldn't be everyone's idea of a fun way to spend a year. But the writer in me found the challenge compelling. Writers are drawn to stories like these, ones where profound sadness and soaring joy wrestle for room on the same page. And my proximity to this tragedy made it a story I couldn't walk away from.

Throughout the writing of this book – from that first email from my publisher Jane Morrow inviting me to submit an idea exploring nature – to the last words I typed on the finished manuscript, my sister Manika has been there guiding my hand.

I'm in no doubt that Manika wanted me to write this book – so much so that many times, as I sat at my desk in the almost-morning unable to continue, I found my fingers tapping out words on the keyboard I was certain hadn't come from me. Manika was a gifted writer and an exacting editor who valued simplicity and brevity. So if you noticed that this book is on the svelte side, this may be why! I know my book has her blessing.

I've never experienced grief like this, and those who've gone through several griefs say each one is unique in its own way. Surviving one does not necessarily prepare you for surviving the next. What I do know is that confronting your grief is better done sooner rather than later. It will haunt you otherwise. Don't be afraid of your grief. Its magnitude only reflects the depth of your love for what you have lost. You can't grieve unless you have loved. And loving is a good thing.

My grief counsellor Wendy Liu has been a godsend. What a generous act it is to hold another's grief. Wendy showed me that grief is personal and universal at the same time. Always remember you are not alone.

To my wonderful urban guides who shared their knowledge, wisdom and passion with me – Phil Angilley, Paul Nicholson, Steve Abbott, Kate Brandis, Branka Spehar, Diego Bonetto, Michael Richards, Ajay Narendra and of course my granddaughter Abbie – I can't thank you enough for your generosity. You all held my heart so tenderly. I tear up just thinking of your infinite kindness.

Acknowledgements

To Jane Morrow and her exceptional team at Murdoch Books – editorial manager Julie Mazur Tribe, my editor Nicola Young, design manager Megan Pigott, designer Trisha Garner and cover artist Clare Walker – where do I begin? You cradled this project as though it were your own child. Thank you for your care, guidance and meticulous attention to detail.

Jennifer Naughton and Beverley Flower at RGM Artists are the wise sounding boards every creative needs in their life. I am so fortunate to have had your counsel and guidance over these last few decades.

A heartfelt thank you to my friends and colleagues who read my book and provided such generous endorsements: I have such admiration for you all and your abundant talents – David Wenham, Kate Ceberano, David George Haskell, Sarah Wilson, Holly Ringland and Chris Taylor.

The Space Between the Stars is also a celebration of my community. There is a camaraderie and togetherness in my hood that lockouts and lockdowns could never destroy. My neighbourhood buddies kept my spirits high – especially when my writing hit the proverbial brick wall as it inevitably did. They were there with a generous ear – or a consoling negroni – despite the confronting times they were each going through. Thank you to Pastors Jon Owen and Graham Long at the Wayside Chapel; Vicki Laing at Laing Real Estate; Steve Summerhayes, our apartment building concierge;

Anna Low at the Potts Point Bookshop, who kept the reading material coming; Nick Stone and Arpana Gehlot at La Bomba and Bar Sopra; Michael Bradley at Melo's Italian; Nigel Nickless and Peter Hurren at Zinc Café; Matt Langdon and Alex Raclet behind the bar at Franca Brasserie; and Barry McDonald at Giorgio's. (I just realised that reads like a really good bar crawl, doesn't it?)

I have a wonderful group of chums who encircle me with just the right mix of goodness and mayhem to keep things interesting. I am so blessed to know you all – Kelly Sloane; Laure, Olivia and Julia Modesti; Tim Petersen and Scottie Monro; Rod and Sandra Kempe; Andrew Cam; Anne Haebich; Ria Voorhaar; Alicia Hollen; Masha Macpherson; Liane Rossler; Prue Clarke and Eric de Cavaignac; Michelle Darlington and Joshi Pittman; David Wenham and Kate Agnew; Darren Dale; Daisy Turnbull; Colin Tate and Matt Fatches; Natalie and Simon Thomas; Dave Gibson; Andrea Jonson; Leigh Sales; George Dodd; Adrian Raschella; Chris Taylor; Jen Wong; Louise Martin; Jon Kingston; Julie Gibbs; Lindsay Olney; and Thea Dikeos. Special thanks to David Wenham, Tim Petersen and Leigh Sales, who were the first to cast their eyes over the completed book. Your feedback gave me confidence that it could help others.

This book wouldn't have seen the light of day if not for my former ABC Radio Sydney manager Mel Withnall. Mel took a gamble approving the months away I needed

Acknowledgements

to finish my writing. There were times when I think we were both unsure I could pull it off or whether I would even return to my radio studio. Mel, thank you for the faith you placed in me, and in the process, for helping me become a more authentic broadcaster. Heartfelt thanks also to my colleagues at *Weekend Nightlife* who kept the show running like clockwork – David Prior, Suzanne Hill, David Murray, Amanda Roberts and Steven Turner.

To my extended family – Sanushka, Tharini and the Mudaliar family; to Sanrisha, Shreya, Darshini, Sonny, Radmila, Suukyi, Dawlay, Bia, Gus and Tony and the Naidoo family; and Arushan and the Pillay family – our veins run thick with the same blood and a shared love for Manika. We will be together again very soon.

To my parents and my sister Suraya who have lost so much, I know your hearts will grow stronger each day. Our family has branched off and coalesced many times as organic organisms do. Now is a time for healing.

To my FitzGerald family – Tim, Nicole, Alice, Jack and Abbie – thank you for bringing the sunshine with you.

No one makes me laugh like my husband Mark. We are each other's impish muses. The creative sparks that fly from our Taurean headbutting fuel our many endeavours. Mark is a free spirit who finds most joy from helping others fly. Thank you for keeping me airborne and for your wise and clever advice on storytelling and structure. You've led me out of the dark on more occasions than I care to remember. Your love is my light.

And finally, and most importantly, to Brent and Alia, whose grief I know is often unbearable. To lose a wife and a mother in this way is unimaginable. Your courage and resilience have amazed me. Know that we hold you close in our thoughts. And also trust that soon the love will outweigh the grief, and when it does a wash of brilliant, shining joy will be waiting for you just around the corner.